ISBN 0-8373-0566-7

C-566 CAREER EXAMINATION SERIES

This is your
PASSBOOK® for...

Campus Security Guard II

Test Preparation Study Guide

Questions & Answers

NLC

NATIONAL LEARNING CORPORATION

Copyright © 2015 by

National Learning Corporation

212 Michael Drive, Syosset, New York 11791

All rights reserved, including the right of reproduction in whole or in part, in any form or by any means, electronic or mechanical, including photocopying, recording, or by any information storage and retrieval system, without permission in writing from the Publisher.

(516) 921-8888
(800) 645-6337
FAX: (516) 921-8743
www.passbooks.com
sales @ passbooks.com
info @ passbooks.com

PRINTED IN THE UNITED STATES OF AMERICA

PASSBOOK®

NOTICE

This book is SOLELY intended for, is sold ONLY to, and its use is RESTRICTED to *individual*, bona fide applicants or candidates who qualify by virtue of having seriously filed applications for appropriate license, certificate, professional and/or promotional advancement, higher school matriculation, scholarship, or other legitimate requirements of educational and/or governmental authorities.

This book is NOT intended for use, class instruction, tutoring, training, duplication, copying, reprinting, excerption, or adaptation, etc., by:

(1) Other publishers

(2) Proprietors and/or Instructors of "Coaching" and/or Preparatory Courses

(3) Personnel and/or Training Divisions of commercial, industrial, and governmental organizations

(4) Schools, colleges, or universities and/or their departments and staffs, including teachers and other personnel

(5) Testing Agencies or Bureaus

(6) Study groups which seek by the purchase of a single volume to copy and/or duplicate and/or adapt this material for use by the group as a whole without having purchased individual volumes for each of the members of the group

(7) Et al.

Such persons would be in violation of appropriate Federal and State statutes.

PROVISION OF LICENSING AGREEMENTS. — Recognized educational commercial, industrial, and governmental institutions and organizations, and others legitimately engaged in educational pursuits, including training, testing, and measurement activities, may address a request for a licensing agreement to the copyright owners, who will determine whether, and under what conditions, including fees and charges, the materials in this book may be used by them. In other words, a licensing facility exists for the legitimate use of the material in this book on other than an individual basis. However, it is asseverated and affirmed here that the material in this book *CANNOT* be used without the receipt of the express permission of such a licensing agreement from the Publishers.

NATIONAL LEARNING CORPORATION
212 Michael Drive
Syosset, New York 11791

Inquiries re licensing agreements should be addressed to:
  The President
  National Learning Corporation
  212 Michael Drive
  Syosset, New York 11791

PASSBOOK® SERIES

THE *PASSBOOK® SERIES* has been created to prepare applicants and candidates for the ultimate academic battlefield – the examination room.

At some time in our lives, each and every one of us may be required to take an examination – for validation, matriculation, admission, qualification, registration, certification, or licensure.

Based on the assumption that every applicant or candidate has met the basic formal educational standards, has taken the required number of courses, and read the necessary texts, the *PASSBOOK® SERIES* furnishes the one special preparation which may assure passing with confidence, instead of failing with insecurity. Examination questions – together with answers – are furnished as the basic vehicle for study so that the mysteries of the examination and its compounding difficulties may be eliminated or diminished by a sure method.

This book is meant to help you pass your examination provided that you qualify and are serious in your objective.

The entire field is reviewed through the huge store of content information which is succinctly presented through a provocative and challenging approach – the question-and-answer method.

A climate of success is established by furnishing the correct answers at the end of each test.

You soon learn to recognize types of questions, forms of questions, and patterns of questioning. You may even begin to anticipate expected outcomes.

You perceive that many questions are repeated or adapted so that you can gain acute insights, which may enable you to score many sure points.

You learn how to confront new questions, or types of questions, and to attack them confidently and work out the correct answers.

You note objectives and emphases, and recognize pitfalls and dangers, so that you may make positive educational adjustments.

Moreover, you are kept fully informed in relation to new concepts, methods, practices, and directions in the field.

You discover that you are actually taking the examination all the time: you are preparing for the examination by "taking" an examination, not by reading extraneous and/or supererogatory textbooks.

In short, this PASSBOOK®, used directedly, should be an important factor in helping you to pass your test.

CAMPUS SECURITY GUARD II

DUTIES
An employee in this class supervises Campus Security Guards I in maintaining public safety and preventing trespassing and property damage at a college campus. Work includes patrolling the campus on foot, bicycle, or by car, performing initial investigations of law violations, responding to fire safety emergencies, and assigning, reviewing and evaluating the work of subordinate personnel. Supervises and participates in traffic control to ensure the safe and orderly passage of vehicles and pedestrians. Supervises crowd control measures at functions which attract large numbers of people; gives direction and assistance to the public. Compiles all investigative material to be passed on to law enforcement agencies. General supervision is received from a Campus Security Guard III and/or administrative supervisor through periodic reports and by observation of the effectiveness of security operations. Does related work as required.

SCOPE OF THE EXAMINATION
The written test will cover knowledge, skills, and/or abilities in such areas as:
1. Reasoning clearly and selecting the proper course of actions in situations involving public safety;
2. Safety and security methods and procedures;
3. Preparing written material;
4. Understanding and interpreting written material; and
5. Supervision.

CAMPUS SECURITY

COMMENTARY

This section describes the structure of the campus security office and appraises its function through an examination of its legal apparatus and by the relationships it has maintained with other components of institutional life.

The findings are based upon research in the legal status of the security office and the authority of the security officer; questions as to the structure, the functioning, and the relationships of the security office; and the assessment of the campus security function and its ability to be supportive to students.

In particular, this summary takes cognizance of the inconsequential role heretofore delegated to the security officer and the significant part he may yet play as the threat to the security of the campus accelerates.

1. The history of the campus security office reflects a variety of service tasks distributed among several functionaries which ultimately came to be housed together. From the early fire-watching days to traffic control and student disorder, it has been a body generally utilized "for" but rarely considered "of" the university. Campus security officers and their predecessors have been long cast in roles of menial activities with minimal responsibilities. Never having attained recognition and legitimacy as a part of the total university community, they continue to exercise an uncertain authority amidst a questioning constituency.
2. The uncertainty that has always surrounded the role of the campus security officer is best evidenced in the limitations placed upon his authority. Until recent years few of the state legislatures bestowed direct arrest authority upon a campus security officer. The authority was obtained derivatively as a result of deputization by the local municipal police department or by the sheriff. Although many state legislatures now permit the governing bodies of higher education, such as the boards of regents, to designate campus security officers with peace officers' authority, deputization continues.
3. This situation exists inasmuch as the authority obtained through the governing bodies is usually of a narrow range and it has not yet had the benefit of adequate court testing and judicial approval. Some few states permit private colleges to obtain similar appointments, generally through application to the governor, but the rule among private colleges has been to rely on deputization for their campus security authority.
4. Among the states requiring mandatory training for entering police officers, several do not yet consider a campus security officer subject to the standards imposed upon peace officers. Moreover, the federal government specifically excludes many campus security officers from the benefits of available training scholarships. Virtually no organized, state-wide specialized training programs for campus security officers are either required under the law or are afforded under state auspices.
5. The law is well established in regard the right of institutions of higher educations to control traffic and parking within their own disciplinary machinery. The courts have upheld the colleges' imposition of reasonable penalties for such violations and have provided the civil court system as an appeal tribunal.
6. Adequate legal precedent exists upon which a campus security officer may enter a residence hall in search of contraband without benefit of a search warrant. The

case law condoning such entry is predicated upon several theories. The major legal premise is that the institution must be afforded the flexibility of access to all buildings in order to properly govern itself. The student is also considered only a temporary occupant of the premises and by his enrollment "waives" certain rights. The privilege of entry is available to administrators and may be delegated to law enforcement officers in the pursuit of a reasonable investigation. The erosion of the "in loco parentis" doctrine and recent judicial pronouncements suggest that the privilege of entry without a warrant may not be arbitrarily invoked.

7. The formalized role of the campus security office in major stress situations such as organized or spontaneous campus disorder is to provide intelligence upon which administrators may make decisions, to serve as liaison with outside police agencies, and to gather evidence for later use against students violating the law. Although the press of events may force campus security officers into confrontation situations, the plans for responding to campus disorders do not generally contemplate such a role. The campus security office's early involvement is aimed primarily at delay so that student personnel officers and the executive officer may have the opportunity to use whatever personal, persuasive influence they can marshal. In the event the institutional executive determines that outside force is necessary, the campus security serves as a communications liaison to interpret the tactical decisions demanded by the outside police agencies in terms of the goals aspired to by the executive.

8. While the complexities of a campus-wide disorder may impose limitations upon the involvement of the security officer, his ability to respond to the normal, foreseeable, routine, enforcement contingencies also remains open to question. The profile of the campus security function discloses many characteristics that suggest only a minimal ability to satisfy ordinary campus needs.

9. Particularly among small institutions and especially private colleges, the training is limited, the equipment is meager, and the advantages over the local police nonexistent. The security force generally lacks specialists within the department, has a minimum of sophisticated equipment, and what little intelligence is available is obtained from outside police sources. Students and female officers are scarcely used and only in short demand.

10. All components of the university recognize that the campus security force most effectively performs the tasks requiring the least specialty training. Building and ground patrol, parking, and traffic control are at the top rank, in that order, while the duties involving criminal investigation and student disorders are the areas least effectively performed.

11. It is apparent to security officers that the presence of larger student bodies, more vehicles on campus, more buildings to patrol, a rise in the individual crime rate, and the potential for disorder arising from student demonstrations call for an increased professional staff.

12. Administrative changes are sought by security officers with almost 60.0 percent favoring a centralized, state-wide coordinating body and almost 70.0 percent requesting a chain of command which would lead directly to the president. None of the other respondent groups (faculty, students, administrators) evinces strong support for these propositions.

13. There is no consensus among the campus groups as to the personnel changes which would most improve performance. The security officers and the administrators ranked salary increase as the top priority personnel change, whereas the students and the faculty selected specialized training in human behavior as their first

choice. Inasmuch as the campus security office services a select clientele in a unique setting, the projected changes need not be weighed against the prototype sought for the law enforcement officer employed to exercise order among the general population.

14. The campus security office has virtually no involvement in policy-making beyond traffic regulations and has little contact in a formal setting with students and faculty. A good working relationship seems to exist with the office of student affairs and other administrators as well as with the outside police agencies.

15. The strong support indicated by all four groups (campus security, faculty, students, and administrators) for the proposition that too few channels of communication exist between the campus security office and the students is evidenced by the lack of security officer participation in student educational programs, by the failure of the campus security office to meet regularly with student committees, and by the security office's absence in the process of establishing student codes of conduct and student discipline procedures. Students involved in off-campus arrests cannot look for security office assistance except to a small extent at schools in the under-10,000 population brackets.

16. Although administrative support for the campus security office as a policy-making body is absent, there is evidence showing regular committee meetings with the office of student affairs and other administration groups. A continuing exchange of information exists with the office of student affairs concerning problem students, and a concurring belief is held by all four groups that the administrators and the office of student affairs would support the action of the campus security office in a disorder situation.

17. The working relationship with administrators also extends to outside police agencies. The local police are available for many manpower and investigative services, and, in some instances, campus violations of the municipal and state law may be handled by security officers within the framework of the school's discipline structure rather than requiring students to face criminal prosecution. Despite the amicable ties between the campus security force and the local police, the security officer joined with the other three groups in unequivocally asserting that the over-reaction by outside police agencies was the occurrence most likely to change an orderly student demonstration into a campus disorder.

18. The aspirations of the campus security officer to contribute to the educational goals of the institution and to participate in its traditional customs finds little of a responsive chord among other components on campus. Although 40.0 percent of the security officers considered the aiding of students in the educational process as an appropriate goal, only 18.0 percent of the students and 6.0 percent of the faculty voiced agreement. The campus security officer viewed himself as the interpreter of the function of police agencies in our society, but the concept had only scattered support with the students and the faculty.

19. There was mixed sentiment toward the campus security officer's enforcement role. Some of the characteristics deemed the antithesis of higher education tradition were attributed to him. For instance, all of the groups identified him with an authoritarian enforcement approach. In addition, 50.0 percent of the student were critical of his use of informers and about 25.0 percent of all groups suggested that uniforms be replaced with civilian-like attire. Despite the 70.0 percent of the security officers seeking increased authority, there was a reluctance to increase campus security authority or to allow participation in student discipline policy-making. The suggestion that the campus security office is a policing agency and as such is

unacceptable to the academic community averaged but a 30.0 percent acceptance among all four groups. While the campus security office was not totally repudiated because of its law enforcement posture, nonetheless it has not been afforded peer status by the other components of the campus society.

20. The anticipation that a supportive relationship can be maintained with students while performing enforcement duties is an unfulfilled expectation. This was apparent to all four groups in their over-70.0 percent recognition that duties such as searching residence halls for contraband are inimical to maintaining a compatible association, and, as well, in their almost 50.0 percent recognition of the stress created in using necessary force against student disorders. Duties involving building and grounds patrol, traffic control, and criminal investigation are performed in less strained settings, permitting a more harmonious relationship.

21. The image of the campus security officer that is transmitted to the student represents order and authority. The uniform, the weapons, and the equipment are synonymous with discipline and control. From the student point of view, the product is not conducive to a mutuality of interest. The absence of joint educational programs and regularly scheduled committee meetings also negates the development of any meaningful interchange. The failure of campus security to offer assistance to students in need of aid as a result of an off-campus arrest may further estrange the two groups. The differential in educational background and age also widens the chasm.

22. Students do not go so far as to state that the campus security officer is too low in the status hierarchy to maintain their respect but they strongly favor supervisory controls such as student ombudsmen and a joint faculty-student committee to review the performance of the campus security officer.

23. The campus security officer as presently constituted is not trained to provide supportive services for students, is not given a status role by the administration which would engender a high regard, and does not participate in policy making or become involved in aspects of the educational process.

24. Little recognition is attainable to the security officer other than that arising from his enforcement activities. There are few if any common grounds existing between him and the student from which a symbiotic relationship may develop.

25. In some few critical areas, the results reflected similar percentage support among the four groups. However, the internal consistency check to determine agreement among the four groups within each institution showed that in only 2 of the 16 selected items were there affirmative responses suggesting consistent agreement within each of the schools. The item of greatest support had 82 of the 89 schools with all four groups agreeing to the truism that the campus security goal is to provide protection for property and person.

Fifty schools had all components in agreement that the overreaction by outside police agencies may change orderly demonstrations into a campus disorder. The other items showed considerably lower internal consistency scores. The diversity of attitude among the component groups that comprise the educational institutions of higher learning and the lack of unanimity within each institution suggest a searching reexamination of the campus security model.

HOW TO TAKE A TEST

I. YOU MUST PASS AN EXAMINATION

A. *WHAT EVERY CANDIDATE SHOULD KNOW*

Examination applicants often ask us for help in preparing for the written test. What can I study in advance? What kinds of questions will be asked? How will the test be given? How will the papers be graded?

As an applicant for a civil service examination, you may be wondering about some of these things. Our purpose here is to suggest effective methods of advance study and to describe civil service examinations.

Your chances for success on this examination can be increased if you know how to prepare. Those "pre-examination jitters" can be reduced if you know what to expect. You can even experience an adventure in good citizenship if you know why civil service exams are given.

B. *WHY ARE CIVIL SERVICE EXAMINATIONS GIVEN?*

Civil service examinations are important to you in two ways. As a citizen, you want public jobs filled by employees who know how to do their work. As a job seeker, you want a fair chance to compete for that job on an equal footing with other candidates. The best-known means of accomplishing this two-fold goal is the competitive examination.

Exams are widely publicized throughout the nation. They may be administered for jobs in federal, state, city, municipal, town or village governments or agencies.

Any citizen may apply, with some limitations, such as the age or residence of applicants. Your experience and education may be reviewed to see whether you meet the requirements for the particular examination. When these requirements exist, they are reasonable and applied consistently to all applicants. Thus, a competitive examination may cause you some uneasiness now, but it is your privilege and safeguard.

C. *HOW ARE CIVIL SERVICE EXAMS DEVELOPED?*

Examinations are carefully written by trained technicians who are specialists in the field known as "psychological measurement," in consultation with recognized authorities in the field of work that the test will cover. These experts recommend the subject matter areas or skills to be tested; only those knowledges or skills important to your success on the job are included. The most reliable books and source materials available are used as references. Together, the experts and technicians judge the difficulty level of the questions.

Test technicians know how to phrase questions so that the problem is clearly stated. Their ethics do not permit "trick" or "catch" questions. Questions may have been tried out on sample groups, or subjected to statistical analysis, to determine their usefulness.

Written tests are often used in combination with performance tests, ratings of training and experience, and oral interviews. All of these measures combine to form the best-known means of finding the right person for the right job.

II. HOW TO PASS THE WRITTEN TEST

A. NATURE OF THE EXAMINATION

To prepare intelligently for civil service examinations, you should know how they differ from school examinations you have taken. In school you were assigned certain definite pages to read or subjects to cover. The examination questions were quite detailed and usually emphasized memory. Civil service exams, on the other hand, try to discover your present ability to perform the duties of a position, plus your potentiality to learn these duties. In other words, a civil service exam attempts to predict how successful you will be. Questions cover such a broad area that they cannot be as minute and detailed as school exam questions.

In the public service similar kinds of work, or positions, are grouped together in one "class." This process is known as *position-classification*. All the positions in a class are paid according to the salary range for that class. One class title covers all of these positions, and they are all tested by the same examination.

B. FOUR BASIC STEPS

1) Study the announcement

How, then, can you know what subjects to study? Our best answer is: "Learn as much as possible about the class of positions for which you've applied." The exam will test the knowledge, skills and abilities needed to do the work.

Your most valuable source of information about the position you want is the official exam announcement. This announcement lists the training and experience qualifications. Check these standards and apply only if you come reasonably close to meeting them.

The brief description of the position in the examination announcement offers some clues to the subjects which will be tested. Think about the job itself. Review the duties in your mind. Can you perform them, or are there some in which you are rusty? Fill in the blank spots in your preparation.

Many jurisdictions preview the written test in the exam announcement by including a section called "Knowledge and Abilities Required," "Scope of the Examination," or some similar heading. Here you will find out specifically what fields will be tested.

2) Review your own background

Once you learn in general what the position is all about, and what you need to know to do the work, ask yourself which subjects you already know fairly well and which need improvement. You may wonder whether to concentrate on improving your strong areas or on building some background in your fields of weakness. When the announcement has specified "some knowledge" or "considerable knowledge," or has used adjectives like "beginning principles of…" or "advanced … methods," you can get a clue as to the number and difficulty of questions to be asked in any given field. More questions, and hence broader coverage, would be included for those subjects which are more important in the work. Now weigh your strengths and weaknesses against the job requirements and prepare accordingly.

3) Determine the level of the position

Another way to tell how intensively you should prepare is to understand the level of the job for which you are applying. Is it the entering level? In other words, is this the position in which beginners in a field of work are hired? Or is it an intermediate or advanced level? Sometimes this is indicated by such words as "Junior" or "Senior" in the class title. Other jurisdictions use Roman numerals to designate the level – Clerk I, Clerk II, for example. The word "Supervisor" sometimes appears in the title. If the level is not indicated by the title, check the description of duties. Will you be working under very close supervision, or will you have responsibility for independent decisions in this work?

4) Choose appropriate study materials

Now that you know the subjects to be examined and the relative amount of each subject to be covered, you can choose suitable study materials. For beginning level jobs, or even advanced ones, if you have a pronounced weakness in some aspect of your training, read a modern, standard textbook in that field. Be sure it is up to date and has general coverage. Such books are normally available at your library, and the librarian will be glad to help you locate one. For entry-level positions, questions of appropriate difficulty are chosen – neither highly advanced questions, nor those too simple. Such questions require careful thought but not advanced training.

If the position for which you are applying is technical or advanced, you will read more advanced, specialized material. If you are already familiar with the basic principles of your field, elementary textbooks would waste your time. Concentrate on advanced textbooks and technical periodicals. Think through the concepts and review difficult problems in your field.

These are all general sources. You can get more ideas on your own initiative, following these leads. For example, training manuals and publications of the government agency which employs workers in your field can be useful, particularly for technical and professional positions. A letter or visit to the government department involved may result in more specific study suggestions, and certainly will provide you with a more definite idea of the exact nature of the position you are seeking.

III. KINDS OF TESTS

Tests are used for purposes other than measuring knowledge and ability to perform specified duties. For some positions, it is equally important to test ability to make adjustments to new situations or to profit from training. In others, basic mental abilities not dependent on information are essential. Questions which test these things may not appear as pertinent to the duties of the position as those which test for knowledge and information. Yet they are often highly important parts of a fair examination. For very general questions, it is almost impossible to help you direct your study efforts. What we can do is to point out some of the more common of these general abilities needed in public service positions and describe some typical questions.

1) General information

Broad, general information has been found useful for predicting job success in some kinds of work. This is tested in a variety of ways, from vocabulary lists to questions about current events. Basic background in some field of work, such as sociology or economics, may be sampled in a group of questions. Often these are principles which have become familiar to most persons through exposure rather than through formal training. It is difficult to advise you how to study for these questions; being alert to the world around you is our best suggestion.

2) Verbal ability

An example of an ability needed in many positions is verbal or language ability. Verbal ability is, in brief, the ability to use and understand words. Vocabulary and grammar tests are typical measures of this ability. Reading comprehension or paragraph interpretation questions are common in many kinds of civil service tests. You are given a paragraph of written material and asked to find its central meaning.

3) Numerical ability
Number skills can be tested by the familiar arithmetic problem, by checking paired lists of numbers to see which are alike and which are different, or by interpreting charts and graphs. In the latter test, a graph may be printed in the test booklet which you are asked to use as the basis for answering questions.

4) Observation
A popular test for law-enforcement positions is the observation test. A picture is shown to you for several minutes, then taken away. Questions about the picture test your ability to observe both details and larger elements.

5) Following directions
In many positions in the public service, the employee must be able to carry out written instructions dependably and accurately. You may be given a chart with several columns, each column listing a variety of information. The questions require you to carry out directions involving the information given in the chart.

6) Skills and aptitudes
Performance tests effectively measure some manual skills and aptitudes. When the skill is one in which you are trained, such as typing or shorthand, you can practice. These tests are often very much like those given in business school or high school courses. For many of the other skills and aptitudes, however, no short-time preparation can be made. Skills and abilities natural to you or that you have developed throughout your lifetime are being tested.

Many of the general questions just described provide all the data needed to answer the questions and ask you to use your reasoning ability to find the answers. Your best preparation for these tests, as well as for tests of facts and ideas, is to be at your physical and mental best. You, no doubt, have your own methods of getting into an exam-taking mood and keeping "in shape." The next section lists some ideas on this subject.

IV. KINDS OF QUESTIONS

Only rarely is the "essay" question, which you answer in narrative form, used in civil service tests. Civil service tests are usually of the short-answer type. Full instructions for answering these questions will be given to you at the examination. But in case this is your first experience with short-answer questions and separate answer sheets, here is what you need to know:

1) Multiple-choice Questions
Most popular of the short-answer questions is the "multiple choice" or "best answer" question. It can be used, for example, to test for factual knowledge, ability to solve problems or judgment in meeting situations found at work.
A multiple-choice question is normally one of three types—
- It can begin with an incomplete statement followed by several possible endings. You are to find the one ending which *best* completes the statement, although some of the others may not be entirely wrong.
- It can also be a complete statement in the form of a question which is answered by choosing one of the statements listed.

- It can be in the form of a problem – again you select the best answer.

Here is an example of a multiple-choice question with a discussion which should give you some clues as to the method for choosing the right answer:

When an employee has a complaint about his assignment, the action which will *best* help him overcome his difficulty is to
- A. discuss his difficulty with his coworkers
- B. take the problem to the head of the organization
- C. take the problem to the person who gave him the assignment
- D. say nothing to anyone about his complaint

In answering this question, you should study each of the choices to find which is best. Consider choice "A" – Certainly an employee may discuss his complaint with fellow employees, but no change or improvement can result, and the complaint remains unresolved. Choice "B" is a poor choice since the head of the organization probably does not know what assignment you have been given, and taking your problem to him is known as "going over the head" of the supervisor. The supervisor, or person who made the assignment, is the person who can clarify it or correct any injustice. Choice "C" is, therefore, correct. To say nothing, as in choice "D," is unwise. Supervisors have and interest in knowing the problems employees are facing, and the employee is seeking a solution to his problem.

2) True/False Questions

The "true/false" or "right/wrong" form of question is sometimes used. Here a complete statement is given. Your job is to decide whether the statement is right or wrong.

SAMPLE: A roaming cell-phone call to a nearby city costs less than a non-roaming call to a distant city.

This statement is wrong, or false, since roaming calls are more expensive.

This is not a complete list of all possible question forms, although most of the others are variations of these common types. You will always get complete directions for answering questions. Be sure you understand *how* to mark your answers – ask questions until you do.

V. RECORDING YOUR ANSWERS

Computer terminals are used more and more today for many different kinds of exams.
For an examination with very few applicants, you may be told to record your answers in the test booklet itself. Separate answer sheets are much more common. If this separate answer sheet is to be scored by machine – and this is often the case – it is highly important that you mark your answers correctly in order to get credit.
An electronic scoring machine is often used in civil service offices because of the speed with which papers can be scored. Machine-scored answer sheets must be marked with a pencil, which will be given to you. This pencil has a high graphite content which responds to the electronic scoring machine. As a matter of fact, stray dots may register as answers, so do not let your pencil rest on the answer sheet while you are pondering the correct answer. Also, if your pencil lead breaks or is otherwise defective, ask for another.

Since the answer sheet will be dropped in a slot in the scoring machine, be careful not to bend the corners or get the paper crumpled.

The answer sheet normally has five vertical columns of numbers, with 30 numbers to a column. These numbers correspond to the question numbers in your test booklet. After each number, going across the page are four or five pairs of dotted lines. These short dotted lines have small letters or numbers above them. The first two pairs may also have a "T" or "F" above the letters. This indicates that the first two pairs only are to be used if the questions are of the true-false type. If the questions are multiple choice, disregard the "T" and "F" and pay attention only to the small letters or numbers.

Answer your questions in the manner of the sample that follows:

32. The largest city in the United States is
    A. Washington, D.C.
    B. New York City
    C. Chicago
    D. Detroit
    E. San Francisco

1) Choose the answer you think is best. (New York City is the largest, so "B" is correct.)
2) Find the row of dotted lines numbered the same as the question you are answering. (Find row number 32)
3) Find the pair of dotted lines corresponding to the answer. (Find the pair of lines under the mark "B.")
4) Make a solid black mark between the dotted lines.

VI. BEFORE THE TEST

Common sense will help you find procedures to follow to get ready for an examination. Too many of us, however, overlook these sensible measures. Indeed, nervousness and fatigue have been found to be the most serious reasons why applicants fail to do their best on civil service tests. Here is a list of reminders:

- Begin your preparation early – Don't wait until the last minute to go scurrying around for books and materials or to find out what the position is all about.
- Prepare continuously – An hour a night for a week is better than an all-night cram session. This has been definitely established. What is more, a night a week for a month will return better dividends than crowding your study into a shorter period of time.
- Locate the place of the exam – You have been sent a notice telling you when and where to report for the examination. If the location is in a different town or otherwise unfamiliar to you, it would be well to inquire the best route and learn something about the building.
- Relax the night before the test – Allow your mind to rest. Do not study at all that night. Plan some mild recreation or diversion; then go to bed early and get a good night's sleep.
- Get up early enough to make a leisurely trip to the place for the test – This way unforeseen events, traffic snarls, unfamiliar buildings, etc. will not upset you.
- Dress comfortably – A written test is not a fashion show. You will be known by number and not by name, so wear something comfortable.

- Leave excess paraphernalia at home – Shopping bags and odd bundles will get in your way. You need bring only the items mentioned in the official notice you received; usually everything you need is provided. Do not bring reference books to the exam. They will only confuse those last minutes and be taken away from you when in the test room.
- Arrive somewhat ahead of time – If because of transportation schedules you must get there very early, bring a newspaper or magazine to take your mind off yourself while waiting.
- Locate the examination room – When you have found the proper room, you will be directed to the seat or part of the room where you will sit. Sometimes you are given a sheet of instructions to read while you are waiting. Do not fill out any forms until you are told to do so; just read them and be prepared.
- Relax and prepare to listen to the instructions
- If you have any physical problem that may keep you from doing your best, be sure to tell the test administrator. If you are sick or in poor health, you really cannot do your best on the exam. You can come back and take the test some other time.

VII. AT THE TEST

The day of the test is here and you have the test booklet in your hand. The temptation to get going is very strong. Caution! There is more to success than knowing the right answers. You must know how to identify your papers and understand variations in the type of short-answer question used in this particular examination. Follow these suggestions for maximum results from your efforts:

1) Cooperate with the monitor

The test administrator has a duty to create a situation in which you can be as much at ease as possible. He will give instructions, tell you when to begin, check to see that you are marking your answer sheet correctly, and so on. He is not there to guard you, although he will see that your competitors do not take unfair advantage. He wants to help you do your best.

2) Listen to all instructions

Don't jump the gun! Wait until you understand all directions. In most civil service tests you get more time than you need to answer the questions. So don't be in a hurry. Read each word of instructions until you clearly understand the meaning. Study the examples, listen to all announcements and follow directions. Ask questions if you do not understand what to do.

3) Identify your papers

Civil service exams are usually identified by number only. You will be assigned a number; you must not put your name on your test papers. Be sure to copy your number correctly. Since more than one exam may be given, copy your exact examination title.

4) Plan your time

Unless you are told that a test is a "speed" or "rate of work" test, speed itself is usually not important. Time enough to answer all the questions will be provided, but this does not mean that you have all day. An overall time limit has been set. Divide the total time (in minutes) by the number of questions to determine the approximate time you have for each question.

5) Do not linger over difficult questions

If you come across a difficult question, mark it with a paper clip (useful to have along) and come back to it when you have been through the booklet. One caution if you do this – be sure to skip a number on your answer sheet as well. Check often to be sure that you have not lost your place and that you are marking in the row numbered the same as the question you are answering.

6) Read the questions

Be sure you know what the question asks! Many capable people are unsuccessful because they failed to *read* the questions correctly.

7) Answer all questions

Unless you have been instructed that a penalty will be deducted for incorrect answers, it is better to guess than to omit a question.

8) Speed tests

It is often better NOT to guess on speed tests. It has been found that on timed tests people are tempted to spend the last few seconds before time is called in marking answers at random – without even reading them – in the hope of picking up a few extra points. To discourage this practice, the instructions may warn you that your score will be "corrected" for guessing. That is, a penalty will be applied. The incorrect answers will be deducted from the correct ones, or some other penalty formula will be used.

9) Review your answers

If you finish before time is called, go back to the questions you guessed or omitted to give them further thought. Review other answers if you have time.

10) Return your test materials

If you are ready to leave before others have finished or time is called, take ALL your materials to the monitor and leave quietly. Never take any test material with you. The monitor can discover whose papers are not complete, and taking a test booklet may be grounds for disqualification.

VIII. EXAMINATION TECHNIQUES

1) Read the general instructions carefully. These are usually printed on the first page of the exam booklet. As a rule, these instructions refer to the timing of the examination; the fact that you should not start work until the signal and must stop work at a signal, etc. If there are any *special* instructions, such as a choice of questions to be answered, make sure that you note this instruction carefully.

2) When you are ready to start work on the examination, that is as soon as the signal has been given, read the instructions to each question booklet, underline any key words or phrases, such as *least, best, outline, describe* and the like. In this way you will tend to answer as requested rather than discover on reviewing your paper that you *listed without describing*, that you selected the *worst* choice rather than the *best* choice, etc.

3) If the examination is of the objective or multiple-choice type – that is, each question will also give a series of possible answers: A, B, C or D, and you are called upon to select the best answer and write the letter next to that answer on your answer paper – it is advisable to start answering each question in turn. There may be anywhere from 50 to 100 such questions in the three or four hours allotted and you can see how much time would be taken if you read through all the questions before beginning to answer any. Furthermore, if you come across a question or group of questions which you know would be difficult to answer, it would undoubtedly affect your handling of all the other questions.

4) If the examination is of the essay type and contains but a few questions, it is a moot point as to whether you should read all the questions before starting to answer any one. Of course, if you are given a choice – say five out of seven and the like – then it is essential to read all the questions so you can eliminate the two that are most difficult. If, however, you are asked to answer all the questions, there may be danger in trying to answer the easiest one first because you may find that you will spend too much time on it. The best technique is to answer the first question, then proceed to the second, etc.

5) Time your answers. Before the exam begins, write down the time it started, then add the time allowed for the examination and write down the time it must be completed, then divide the time available somewhat as follows:
    - If 3-1/2 hours are allowed, that would be 210 minutes. If you have 80 objective-type questions, that would be an average of 2-1/2 minutes per question. Allow yourself no more than 2 minutes per question, or a total of 160 minutes, which will permit about 50 minutes to review.
    - If for the time allotment of 210 minutes there are 7 essay questions to answer, that would average about 30 minutes a question. Give yourself only 25 minutes per question so that you have about 35 minutes to review.

6) The most important instruction is to *read each question* and make sure you know what is wanted. The second most important instruction is to *time yourself properly* so that you answer every question. The third most important instruction is to *answer every question*. Guess if you have to but include something for each question. Remember that you will receive no credit for a blank and will probably receive some credit if you write something in answer to an essay question. If you guess a letter – say "B" for a multiple-choice question – you may have guessed right. If you leave a blank as an answer to a multiple-choice question, the examiners may respect your feelings but it will not add a point to your score. Some exams may penalize you for wrong answers, so in such cases *only*, you may not want to guess unless you have some basis for your answer.

7) Suggestions
    a. Objective-type questions
        1. Examine the question booklet for proper sequence of pages and questions
        2. Read all instructions carefully
        3. Skip any question which seems too difficult; return to it after all other questions have been answered
        4. Apportion your time properly; do not spend too much time on any single question or group of questions

5. Note and underline key words – *all, most, fewest, least, best, worst, same, opposite,* etc.
6. Pay particular attention to negatives
7. Note unusual option, e.g., unduly long, short, complex, different or similar in content to the body of the question
8. Observe the use of "hedging" words – *probably, may, most likely,* etc.
9. Make sure that your answer is put next to the same number as the question
10. Do not second-guess unless you have good reason to believe the second answer is definitely more correct
11. Cross out original answer if you decide another answer is more accurate; do not erase until you are ready to hand your paper in
12. Answer all questions; guess unless instructed otherwise
13. Leave time for review

b. Essay questions
1. Read each question carefully
2. Determine exactly what is wanted. Underline key words or phrases.
3. Decide on outline or paragraph answer
4. Include many different points and elements unless asked to develop any one or two points or elements
5. Show impartiality by giving pros and cons unless directed to select one side only
6. Make and write down any assumptions you find necessary to answer the questions
7. Watch your English, grammar, punctuation and choice of words
8. Time your answers; don't crowd material

8) Answering the essay question

Most essay questions can be answered by framing the specific response around several key words or ideas. Here are a few such key words or ideas:

M's: manpower, materials, methods, money, management
P's: purpose, program, policy, plan, procedure, practice, problems, pitfalls, personnel, public relations

a. Six basic steps in handling problems:
1. Preliminary plan and background development
2. Collect information, data and facts
3. Analyze and interpret information, data and facts
4. Analyze and develop solutions as well as make recommendations
5. Prepare report and sell recommendations
6. Install recommendations and follow up effectiveness

b. Pitfalls to avoid
1. *Taking things for granted* – A statement of the situation does not necessarily imply that each of the elements is necessarily true; for example, a complaint may be invalid and biased so that all that can be taken for granted is that a complaint has been registered

2. *Considering only one side of a situation* – Wherever possible, indicate several alternatives and then point out the reasons you selected the best one
3. *Failing to indicate follow up* – Whenever your answer indicates action on your part, make certain that you will take proper follow-up action to see how successful your recommendations, procedures or actions turn out to be
4. *Taking too long in answering any single question* – Remember to time your answers properly

IX. AFTER THE TEST

Scoring procedures differ in detail among civil service jurisdictions although the general principles are the same. Whether the papers are hand-scored or graded by machine we have described, they are nearly always graded by number. That is, the person who marks the paper knows only the number – never the name – of the applicant. Not until all the papers have been graded will they be matched with names. If other tests, such as training and experience or oral interview ratings have been given, scores will be combined. Different parts of the examination usually have different weights. For example, the written test might count 60 percent of the final grade, and a rating of training and experience 40 percent. In many jurisdictions, veterans will have a certain number of points added to their grades.

After the final grade has been determined, the names are placed in grade order and an eligible list is established. There are various methods for resolving ties between those who get the same final grade – probably the most common is to place first the name of the person whose application was received first. Job offers are made from the eligible list in the order the names appear on it. You will be notified of your grade and your rank as soon as all these computations have been made. This will be done as rapidly as possible.

People who are found to meet the requirements in the announcement are called "eligibles." Their names are put on a list of eligible candidates. An eligible's chances of getting a job depend on how high he stands on this list and how fast agencies are filling jobs from the list.

When a job is to be filled from a list of eligibles, the agency asks for the names of people on the list of eligibles for that job. When the civil service commission receives this request, it sends to the agency the names of the three people highest on this list. Or, if the job to be filled has specialized requirements, the office sends the agency the names of the top three persons who meet these requirements from the general list.

The appointing officer makes a choice from among the three people whose names were sent to him. If the selected person accepts the appointment, the names of the others are put back on the list to be considered for future openings.

That is the rule in hiring from all kinds of eligible lists, whether they are for typist, carpenter, chemist, or something else. For every vacancy, the appointing officer has his choice of any one of the top three eligibles on the list. This explains why the person whose name is on top of the list sometimes does not get an appointment when some of the persons lower on the list do. If the appointing officer chooses the second or third eligible, the No. 1 eligible does not get a job at once, but stays on the list until he is appointed or the list is terminated.

X. HOW TO PASS THE INTERVIEW TEST

The examination for which you applied requires an oral interview test. You have already taken the written test and you are now being called for the interview test – the final part of the formal examination.

You may think that it is not possible to prepare for an interview test and that there are no procedures to follow during an interview. Our purpose is to point out some things you can do in advance that will help you and some good rules to follow and pitfalls to avoid while you are being interviewed.

What is an interview supposed to test?

The written examination is designed to test the technical knowledge and competence of the candidate; the oral is designed to evaluate intangible qualities, not readily measured otherwise, and to establish a list showing the relative fitness of each candidate – as measured against his competitors – for the position sought. Scoring is not on the basis of "right" and "wrong," but on a sliding scale of values ranging from "not passable" to "outstanding." As a matter of fact, it is possible to achieve a relatively low score without a single "incorrect" answer because of evident weakness in the qualities being measured.

Occasionally, an examination may consist entirely of an oral test – either an individual or a group oral. In such cases, information is sought concerning the technical knowledges and abilities of the candidate, since there has been no written examination for this purpose. More commonly, however, an oral test is used to supplement a written examination.

Who conducts interviews?

The composition of oral boards varies among different jurisdictions. In nearly all, a representative of the personnel department serves as chairman. One of the members of the board may be a representative of the department in which the candidate would work. In some cases, "outside experts" are used, and, frequently, a businessman or some other representative of the general public is asked to serve. Labor and management or other special groups may be represented. The aim is to secure the services of experts in the appropriate field.

However the board is composed, it is a good idea (and not at all improper or unethical) to ascertain in advance of the interview who the members are and what groups they represent. When you are introduced to them, you will have some idea of their backgrounds and interests, and at least you will not stutter and stammer over their names.

What should be done before the interview?

While knowledge about the board members is useful and takes some of the surprise element out of the interview, there is other preparation which is more substantive. It *is* possible to prepare for an oral interview – in several ways:

1) Keep a copy of your application and review it carefully before the interview

This may be the only document before the oral board, and the starting point of the interview. Know what education and experience you have listed there, and the sequence and dates of all of it. Sometimes the board will ask you to review the highlights of your experience for them; you should not have to hem and haw doing it.

2) Study the class specification and the examination announcement

Usually, the oral board has one or both of these to guide them. The qualities, characteristics or knowledges required by the position sought are stated in these documents. They offer valuable clues as to the nature of the oral interview. For example, if the job involves supervisory responsibilities, the announcement will usually indicate that knowledge of modern supervisory methods and the qualifications of the candidate as a supervisor will be tested. If so, you can expect such questions, frequently in the form of a hypothetical situation which you are expected to solve. NEVER go into an oral without knowledge of the duties and responsibilities of the job you seek.

3) Think through each qualification required
Try to visualize the kind of questions you would ask if you were a board member. How well could you answer them? Try especially to appraise your own knowledge and background in each area, *measured against the job sought*, and identify any areas in which you are weak. Be critical and realistic – do not flatter yourself.

4) Do some general reading in areas in which you feel you may be weak
For example, if the job involves supervision and your past experience has NOT, some general reading in supervisory methods and practices, particularly in the field of human relations, might be useful. Do NOT study agency procedures or detailed manuals. The oral board will be testing your understanding and capacity, not your memory.

5) Get a good night's sleep and watch your general health and mental attitude
You will want a clear head at the interview. Take care of a cold or any other minor ailment, and of course, no hangovers.

What should be done on the day of the interview?
Now comes the day of the interview itself. Give yourself plenty of time to get there. Plan to arrive somewhat ahead of the scheduled time, particularly if your appointment is in the fore part of the day. If a previous candidate fails to appear, the board might be ready for you a bit early. By early afternoon an oral board is almost invariably behind schedule if there are many candidates, and you may have to wait. Take along a book or magazine to read, or your application to review, but leave any extraneous material in the waiting room when you go in for your interview. In any event, relax and compose yourself.

The matter of dress is important. The board is forming impressions about you – from your experience, your manners, your attitude, and your appearance. Give your personal appearance careful attention. Dress your best, but not your flashiest. Choose conservative, appropriate clothing, and be sure it is immaculate. This is a business interview, and your appearance should indicate that you regard it as such. Besides, being well groomed and properly dressed will help boost your confidence.

Sooner or later, someone will call your name and escort you into the interview room. *This is it.* From here on you are on your own. It is too late for any more preparation. But remember, you asked for this opportunity to prove your fitness, and you are here because your request was granted.

What happens when you go in?
The usual sequence of events will be as follows: The clerk (who is often the board stenographer) will introduce you to the chairman of the oral board, who will introduce you to the other members of the board. Acknowledge the introductions before you sit down. Do not be surprised if you find a microphone facing you or a stenotypist sitting by. Oral interviews are usually recorded in the event of an appeal or other review.

Usually the chairman of the board will open the interview by reviewing the highlights of your education and work experience from your application – primarily for the benefit of the other members of the board, as well as to get the material into the record. Do not interrupt or comment unless there is an error or significant misinterpretation; if that is the case, do not hesitate. But do not quibble about insignificant matters. Also, he will usually ask you some question about your education, experience or your present job – partly to get you to start talking and to establish the interviewing "rapport." He may start the actual questioning, or turn it over to one of the other members. Frequently, each member undertakes the questioning on a particular area, one in which he is perhaps most competent, so you can expect each member to participate in the examination. Because time is limited, you may also expect some rather abrupt switches in the direction the questioning takes, so do not be upset by it. Normally, a board member will not pursue a single line of questioning unless he discovers a particular strength or weakness.

After each member has participated, the chairman will usually ask whether any member has any further questions, then will ask you if you have anything you wish to add. Unless you are expecting this question, it may floor you. Worse, it may start you off on an extended, extemporaneous speech. The board is not usually seeking more information. The question is principally to offer you a last opportunity to present further qualifications or to indicate that you have nothing to add. So, if you feel that a significant qualification or characteristic has been overlooked, it is proper to point it out in a sentence or so. Do not compliment the board on the thoroughness of their examination – they have been sketchy, and you know it. If you wish, merely say, "No thank you, I have nothing further to add." This is a point where you can "talk yourself out" of a good impression or fail to present an important bit of information. Remember, *you close the interview yourself.*

The chairman will then say, "That is all, Mr. _____, thank you." Do not be startled; the interview is over, and quicker than you think. Thank him, gather your belongings and take your leave. Save your sigh of relief for the other side of the door.

How to put your best foot forward

Throughout this entire process, you may feel that the board individually and collectively is trying to pierce your defenses, seek out your hidden weaknesses and embarrass and confuse you. Actually, this is not true. They are obliged to make an appraisal of your qualifications for the job you are seeking, and they want to see you in your best light. Remember, they must interview all candidates and a non-cooperative candidate may become a failure in spite of their best efforts to bring out his qualifications. Here are 15 suggestions that will help you:

1) **Be natural – Keep your attitude confident, not cocky**

If you are not confident that you can do the job, do not expect the board to be. Do not apologize for your weaknesses, try to bring out your strong points. The board is interested in a positive, not negative, presentation. Cockiness will antagonize any board member and make him wonder if you are covering up a weakness by a false show of strength.

2) **Get comfortable, but don't lounge or sprawl**

Sit erectly but not stiffly. A careless posture may lead the board to conclude that you are careless in other things, or at least that you are not impressed by the importance of the occasion. Either conclusion is natural, even if incorrect. Do not fuss with your clothing, a pencil or an ashtray. Your hands may occasionally be useful to emphasize a point; do not let them become a point of distraction.

3) **Do not wisecrack or make small talk**

This is a serious situation, and your attitude should show that you consider it as such. Further, the time of the board is limited – they do not want to waste it, and neither should you.

4) Do not exaggerate your experience or abilities
In the first place, from information in the application or other interviews and sources, the board may know more about you than you think. Secondly, you probably will not get away with it. An experienced board is rather adept at spotting such a situation, so do not take the chance.

5) If you know a board member, do not make a point of it, yet do not hide it
Certainly you are not fooling him, and probably not the other members of the board. Do not try to take advantage of your acquaintanceship – it will probably do you little good.

6) Do not dominate the interview
Let the board do that. They will give you the clues – do not assume that you have to do all the talking. Realize that the board has a number of questions to ask you, and do not try to take up all the interview time by showing off your extensive knowledge of the answer to the first one.

7) Be attentive
You only have 20 minutes or so, and you should keep your attention at its sharpest throughout. When a member is addressing a problem or question to you, give him your undivided attention. Address your reply principally to him, but do not exclude the other board members.

8) Do not interrupt
A board member may be stating a problem for you to analyze. He will ask you a question when the time comes. Let him state the problem, and wait for the question.

9) Make sure you understand the question
Do not try to answer until you are sure what the question is. If it is not clear, restate it in your own words or ask the board member to clarify it for you. However, do not haggle about minor elements.

10) Reply promptly but not hastily
A common entry on oral board rating sheets is "candidate responded readily," or "candidate hesitated in replies." Respond as promptly and quickly as you can, but do not jump to a hasty, ill-considered answer.

11) Do not be peremptory in your answers
A brief answer is proper – but do not fire your answer back. That is a losing game from your point of view. The board member can probably ask questions much faster than you can answer them.

12) Do not try to create the answer you think the board member wants
He is interested in what kind of mind you have and how it works – not in playing games. Furthermore, he can usually spot this practice and will actually grade you down on it.

13) Do not switch sides in your reply merely to agree with a board member
Frequently, a member will take a contrary position merely to draw you out and to see if you are willing and able to defend your point of view. Do not start a debate, yet do not surrender a good position. If a position is worth taking, it is worth defending.

14) Do not be afraid to admit an error in judgment if you are shown to be wrong

The board knows that you are forced to reply without any opportunity for careful consideration. Your answer may be demonstrably wrong. If so, admit it and get on with the interview.

15) Do not dwell at length on your present job

The opening question may relate to your present assignment. Answer the question but do not go into an extended discussion. You are being examined for a *new* job, not your present one. As a matter of fact, try to phrase ALL your answers in terms of the job for which you are being examined.

Basis of Rating

Probably you will forget most of these "do's" and "don'ts" when you walk into the oral interview room. Even remembering them all will not ensure you a passing grade. Perhaps you did not have the qualifications in the first place. But remembering them will help you to put your best foot forward, without treading on the toes of the board members.

Rumor and popular opinion to the contrary notwithstanding, an oral board wants you to make the best appearance possible. They know you are under pressure – but they also want to see how you respond to it as a guide to what your reaction would be under the pressures of the job you seek. They will be influenced by the degree of poise you display, the personal traits you show and the manner in which you respond.

ABOUT THIS BOOK

This book contains tests divided into Examination Sections. Go through each test, answering every question in the margin. We have also attached a sample answer sheet at the back of the book that can be removed and used. At the end of each test look at the answer key and check your answers. On the ones you got wrong, look at the right answer choice and learn. Do not fill in the answers first. Do not memorize the questions and answers, but understand the answer and principles involved. On your test, the questions will likely be different from the samples. Questions are changed and new ones added. If you understand these past questions you should have success with any changes that arise. Tests may consist of several types of questions. We have additional books on each subject should more study be advisable or necessary for you. Finally, the more you study, the better prepared you will be. This book is intended to be the last thing you study before you walk into the examination room. Prior study of relevant texts is also recommended. NLC publishes some of these in our Fundamental Series. Knowledge and good sense are important factors in passing your exam. Good luck also helps. So now study this Passbook, absorb the material contained within and take that knowledge into the examination. Then do your best to pass that exam.

EXAMINATION SECTION

EXAMINATION SECTION
TEST 1

DIRECTIONS: Each question or incomplete statement is followed by several suggested answers or completions. Select the one that BEST answers the question or completes the statement. *PRINT THE LETTER OF THE CORRECT ANSWER IN THE SPACE AT THE RIGHT.*

1. Which of the following is the LEAST important factor to consider in surveying the physical layout of a building for traffic flow?　　1.____

    A. Location of windows
    B. Number of entrances
    C. Number of exits
    D. Location of first aid rooms

2. The major purpose of any security program in a large organization is to prevent unlawful acts.　　2.____
   If adequate patrol coverage is provided at a given location, it is MOST likely that

    A. crimes will not be committed
    B. undesirables will not enter the building
    C. unlawful acts will increase in the long run
    D. there will be less opportunity to commit a crime

3. The MOST frequent cause of fires in public facilities is　　3.____

    A. incinerators　　　　　　　　B. vandalism
    C. electrical sources　　　　　D. smoking on the job

4. After bomb threats are received, it is sometimes necessary to evacuate a facility. How long BEFORE the threatened time of explosion should a facility be evacuated?　　4.____
   At least _____ minutes.

    A. 15　　　　B. 25　　　　C. 50　　　　D. 60

5. Once a facility is evacuated because of a bomb threat, how much time should pass before the public and employees are allowed to enter the building?　　5.____
   _____ minutes.

    A. 10　　　　B. 20　　　　C. 40　　　　D. 60

6. Of the following locations in public buildings, the one which is the LEAST likely place for bombs to be planted is in　　6.____

    A. storerooms　　　　　　B. bathrooms
    C. cafeterias　　　　　　　D. waste receptacles

7. The one of the following that is the surest means of establishing positive identification of someone entering a facility is by　　7.____

    A. personal recognition　　　B. I.D. badge
    C. social security card　　　　D. driver's license

8. The one of the following which most probably would NOT be included in a police record report concerning an incident at a facility is the

   A. name of complainant or injured party
   B. name of the investigating officer
   C. statement of each witness
   D. religion of complainant or injured party

9. Preventing trouble is one of the primary concerns of special officers.
   When dealing with unruly groups of people who threaten to become violent, which of the following is a measure which should NOT be taken?

   A. Maintain close surveillance of such groups
   B. Try to contact the leaders of the group regardless of their militancy
   C. Keep the officer force alerted
   D. Have the officer force deal aggressively with provocations

10. Of the following, the MOST important factor to consider in the deployment of officers dealing with a client population is the officers' ability to

    A. remain calm   B. look stern
    C. evaluate personality   D. take a firm stand

11. Assume that an offender is struggling with a group of officers who are trying to arrest him.
    What force, if any, can be used to overcome this resistance?

    A. The amount of force acceptable to the public
    B. The amount of force necessary to restrain the offender and protect the officers
    C. Any amount of force that is acceptable to the officers at the scene
    D. No force may be used until the police arrive

12. Assume that a fire is discovered at your work location. The one of the following actions which would be INAPPROPRIATE for you to take is to

    A. notify the telephone operator
    B. station a reliable person at the entrance
    C. open all windows and doors in the area
    D. start evacuating the area

13. If a person has an object caught in his throat or air passage but is breathing adequately, which one of the following should you do?

    A. Probe for the object
    B. Force him to drink water
    C. Lay him over your arm and slap him between the shoulder blades
    D. Allow him to cough and to assume the position he finds most comfortable

14. The one of the following methods which should NOT be used to report a fire is to

    A. call 911
    B. pull the handle in the red box on the street corner
    C. call the fire department county numbers listed in each county directory
    D. call 411

15. Assume that an officer, alone in a building at night, smells the strong odor of cooking or heating gas. In addition to airing the building and making sure that he is not overcome, it would be BEST for the officer to call

    A. his superior at his home and ask for instructions
    B. for a plumber from the department of public works
    C. 911 for police and fire help
    D. the emergency number at Con Edison

16. Of the following situations, the one that is MOST dangerous for an officer is when he

    A. investigates suspicious persons and circumstances
    B. finds a burglary in progress or pursues burglary suspects
    C. attempts an arrest or finds a robbery in progress
    D. patrols on the overnight shift

17. An officer on security patrol generally should spend MOST of his time

    A. checking doors and locks
    B. helping the public and answering questions
    C. chasing criminals and looking for clues
    D. writing reports on unusual incidents

18. The one of the following that is an ACCEPTABLE way to arrest a person is to

    A. tell him to report to the nearest police precinct
    B. send a summons to his permanent address
    C. tell him in person that he is under arrest
    D. show him handcuffs and ask him to come along

19. A carbon dioxide fire extinguisher is BEST suited for extinguishing _____ fires.

    A. paper   B. rag   C. rubbish   D. grease

20. A pressurized water or soda-acid fire extinguisher is BEST suited for extinguishing _____ fires.

    A. wood   B. gasoline
    C. electrical   D. magnesium

21. The one of the following statements that does NOT apply to the use of handcuffs is that they

    A. are used as temporary restraining devices
    B. eliminate the need for vigilance
    C. cannot be opened without keys
    D. are used to secure a violent person

22. The one of the following that is GENERALLY a crime against the person is

    A. trespass   B. burglary   C. robbery   D. arson

23. Of the following, the SAFEST way of escape from an office in a burning building is generally the

   A. stairway
   B. rooftop
   C. passenger elevator
   D. freight elevator

24. In attempting to control a possible riot situation, an officer pushed his way into a crowd gathered outside the building and tried to cause confusion by arguing with members of the group.
   This procedure NORMALLY is considered

   A. *desirable;* any violence that occurs will remain outside the building
   B. *desirable;* the crowd will break into smaller groups and disperse
   C. *undesirable;* to maintain control of the situation, the officer must not become part of the crowd
   D. *undesirable;* the supervisor should stay clear of the scene

25. Which one of the following is MOST effective in making officers more safety-minded?

   A. Maintaining an up-to-date library of the latest safety literature
   B. Reading daily safety bulletins at roll-call
   C. Holding informal group safety meetings periodically
   D. Offering prizes for good safety slogans and displays

KEY (CORRECT ANSWERS)

1. A	11. B
2. D	12. C
3. C	13. D
4. A	14. D
5. D	15. D
6. C	16. C
7. A	17. A
8. D	18. C
9. D	19. D
10. A	20. A

21. B
22. C
23. A
24. C
25. C

TEST 2

DIRECTIONS: Each question or incomplete statement is followed by several suggested answers or completions. Select the one that BEST answers the question or completes the statement. *PRINT THE LETTER OF THE CORRECT ANSWER IN THE SPACE AT THE RIGHT.*

1. Assume that an angry crowd of some 75 to 100 people has built up in one of the hallways of a center and that only one superior officer and two subordinate officers are on duty in the building. A glass panel in one of the stairway doors has just been broken under the pressure of the crowd and a bench has been hurled down a flight of stairs. The one of the following actions that the superior officer SHOULD take in this situation is to

    A. push his way into the crowd and try to reason with them
    B. order the two other officers to try to quiet the crowd
    C. call the police on 911 and meet them outside the building
    D. do nothing at this point in order to avoid a riot

1.____

2. One of the duties and responsibilities of a supervisor is to test the knowledge of the officers concerning their post conditions.
This should be done if the officer's assignment is

    A. fixed only
    B. roving only
    C. roving only in a troublesome spot
    D. either fixed or roving

2.____

3. An officer discovers early one morning that an office in the building he guards has been burglarized.
Of the following, it is important for the officer to FIRST

    A. go through the building and look for suspects
    B. call the police and protect the area and whatever evidence exists until they arrive
    C. allow people into their offices as they come to work
    D. examine, sort, and handle all evidence before the police get there

3.____

4. Assume that two officers are interrogating one suspect. How should these officers position themselves during the interrogation?

    A. One officer should stand on either side of the suspect.
    B. One officer should stand to the right of the suspect, and the other officer should stand behind the suspect.
    C. Both officers should stand to the right of the suspect.
    D. One officer should stand to the right of the suspect, and the other officer should stand in front of the suspect.

4.____

5. A witness who takes an oath to testify truly and who states as true any matter which he knows to be false is guilty of

    A. perjury   B. libel   C. slander   D. fraud

5.____

6. An officer checking a substance suspected of containing narcotics should GENERALLY

   A. taste it in small amounts
   B. send it to a laboratory for analysis
   C. smell it for its distinctive odor
   D. examine it for its unusual texture

7. A certain center is situated in an area where frequent outbreaks of hostilities seem to be focused on the center itself.
Which of the following BEST explains why the center may be a target for hostile acts?
It

   A. serves community needs
   B. represents governmental authority
   C. represents all ethnic groups
   D. serves as a neutral battlefield

8. An officer often deals with people who might be addicted to drugs.
The one of the following symptoms which is NOT generally an indication of drug addiction is

   A. dilation of the eye pupils
   B. frequent yawning and sneezing
   C. a deep, rasping cough
   D. continual itching of the arms and legs

9. In emergency situations, panic will MOST probably occur when people are

   A. unexpectedly confronted with a terrorizing condition from which there appears to be no escape
   B. angry and violent
   C. anxious about circumstances which are not obvious, easily visible or within the immediate area
   D. familiar with the effects of the emergency

10. The one of the following actions on the part of a person that would NOT be considered *resisting arrest* is

    A. retreating and running away
    B. saying, *You can't arrest me*
    C. pushing the officer aside
    D. pulling away from an officer's grasp

11. Which of the following items would NOT be considered an APPROPRIATE item of uniform for an officer to wear while on duty?

    A. Reefer type overcoat
    B. Leather laced shoes with flat soles
    C. White socks
    D. Cap cover with cap device displayed

12. What can happen to an officer if the leather thong on his night stick is NOT twisted correctly?
The

   A. baton may be taken out of the officer's hand
   B. officer's wrist may be broken
   C. leather will tear more easily
   D. officer's arm may be injured

13. The one of the following kinds of information which SHOULD be included in the log book is

   A. any important matter of police information
   B. an item noted in Standard Operating Procedures only
   C. everything of general interest
   D. a crime or offense only

14. While on patrol at your work location, you receive a call that an assault has taken place. Upon your arrival at the scene, the victim, who has severe lacerations, informs you that the assailant ran into a nearby basement.
After apprehending the suspect, the type of search you should conduct is a _____ search.

   A. wall   B. frisk   C. body   D. strip

15. A tactical force is valuable in MOST emergency situations PRIMARILY because of its

   A. location   B. morale
   C. flexibility   D. size

16. An officer should be encouraged to talk easily and frankly when he is dealing with his superior.
In order to encourage such free communication, it would be MOST appropriate for a superior to behave in a(n)

   A. *sincere* manner; assure the officer that you will deal with him honestly and openly
   B. *official* manner; you are a superior officer and must always act formally with subordinates
   C. *investigative* manner; you must probe and question to get to a basis of trust
   D. *unemotional* manner; the officer's emotions and background should play no part in your dealings with him

17. Research findings show that an increase in free communication within an agency GENERALLY results in which one of the following?

   A. Improved morale and productivity
   B. Increased promotional opportunities
   C. An increase in authority
   D. A spirit of honesty

18. Assume that you are a superior officer and your superiors have given you a new arrest procedure to be followed. Before passing this information on to your subordinates, the one of the following actions that you should take FIRST is to

    A. ask your superiors to send out a memorandum to the entire staff
    B. clarify the procedure in your own mind
    C. set up a training course to provide instructions on the new procedure
    D. write a memorandum to your subordinates

19. Communication is necessary for an organization to be effective.
    The one of the following which is LEAST important for most communication systems is that

    A. messages are sent quickly and directly to the person who needs them to operate
    B. information should be conveyed understandably and accurately
    C. the method used to transmit information should be kept secret so that security can be maintained
    D. senders of messages must know how their messages were received and acted upon

20. Which one of the following is the CHIEF advantage of listening willingly to subordinate officers and encouraging them to talk freely and honestly?
    It

    A. reveals to superiors the degree to which ideas that are passed down are accepted by subordinates
    B. reduces the participation of subordinates in the operation of the department
    C. encourages officers to try for promotion
    D. enables officers to learn about security leaks on the part of officials

21. A superior may be informed through either oral or written reports.
    Which one of the following is an ADVANTAGE of using oral reports?

    A. There is no need for a formal record of the report.
    B. An exact duplicate of the report is not easily transmitted to others.
    C. A good oral report requires little time for preparation.
    D. An oral report involves two-way communication between a subordinate and his superior.

22. Of the following, the MOST important reason why officers should communicate effectively with the public is to

    A. improve the public's understanding of information that is important for them to know
    B. establish a friendly relationship
    C. obtain information about the kinds of people who come to the center
    D. convince the public that services are adequate

23. Officers should generally NOT use phrases like *too hard, too easy,* and *a lot* principally because such phrases

    A. may be offensive to some minority groups
    B. are too informal

C. mean different things to different people
D. are difficult to remember

24. The ability to communicate clearly and concisely is an important element in effective leadership.
Which of the following statements about oral and written communication is GENERALLY true?

   A. Oral communication is more time-consuming.
   B. Written communication is more likely to be misinterpreted.
   C. Oral communication is useful only in emergencies.
   D. Written communication is useful mainly when giving information to fewer than twenty people.

25. Rumors can often have harmful and disruptive effects on an organization.
Which one of the following is the BEST way to prevent rumors from becoming a problem?

   A. Refuse to act on rumors, thereby making them less believable
   B. Increase the amount of information passed along by the *grapevine*
   C. Distribute as much factual information as possible
   D. Provide training in report writing

KEY (CORRECT ANSWERS)

1.	C	11.	C
2.	D	12.	A
3.	B	13.	A
4.	B	14.	A
5.	A	15.	C
6.	B	16.	A
7.	B	17.	A
8.	C	18.	B
9.	A	19.	C
10.	B	20.	A

21. D
22. A
23. C
24. B
25. C

EXAMINATION SECTION
TEST 1

DIRECTIONS: Each question or incomplete statement is followed by several suggested answers or completions. Select the one that BEST answers the question or completes the statement. *PRINT THE LETTER OF THE CORRECT ANSWER IN THE SPACE AT THE RIGHT.*

1. Of the following, the MOST important single factor in any building security program is 1.____

    A. a fool-proof employee identification system
    B. an effective control of entrances and exits
    C. bright illumination of all outside areas
    D. clearly marking public and non-public areas

2. There is general agreement that the BEST criterion of what is a good physical security system in a large public building is 2.____

    A. the number of uniformed officers needed to patrol sensitive areas
    B. how successfully the system prevents rather than detects violations
    C. the number of persons caught in the act of committing criminal offenses
    D. how successfully the system succeeds in maintaining good public relations

3. Which one of the following statements most correctly expresses the CHIEF reason why women were originally made eligible for appointment to the position of officer? 3.____

    A. Certain tasks in security protection can be performed best by assigning women.
    B. More women than men are available to fill many vacancies in this position.
    C. The government wants more women in law enforcement because of their better attendance records.
    D. Women can no longer be barred from any government jobs because of sex.

4. The MOST BASIC purpose of patrol by officers is to 4.____

    A. eliminate as much as possible the opportunity for successful misconduct
    B. investigate criminal complaints and accident cases
    C. give prompt assistance to employees and citizens in distress or requesting their help
    D. take persons into custody who commit criminal offenses against persons and property

5. The highest quality of patrol service is MOST generally obtained by 5.____

    A. frequently changing the post assignments of each officer
    B. assigning officers to posts of equal size
    C. assigning problem officers to the least desirable posts
    D. assigning the same officers to the same posts

6. The one of the following requirements which is MOST essential to the successful performance of patrol duty by individual officers is their 6.____

    A. ability to communicate effectively with higher-level officers
    B. prompt signalling according to a prescribed schedule to insure post coverages at all times

C. knowledge of post conditions and post hazards
D. willingness to cover large areas during periods of critical manpower shortages

7. Officers on patrol are constantly warned to be on the alert for suspicious persons, actions, and circumstances.
With this in mind, a senior officer should emphasize the need for them to

   A. be cautious and suspicious when dealing officially with any civilian regardless of the latter's overt actions or the circumstances surrounding his dealings with the police
   B. keep looking for the unusual persons, actions, and circumstances on their posts and pay less attention to the usual
   C. take aggressive police action immediately against any unusual person or condition detected on their posts, regardless of any other circumstances
   D. become thoroughly familiar with the usual on their posts so as to be better able to detect the unusual

8. Of primary importance in the safeguarding of property from theft is a good central lock and key issuance and control system.
Which one of the following recommendations about maintaining such a control system would be LEAST acceptable?

   A. In selecting locks to be used for the various gates, building, and storage areas, consideration should be given to the amount of security desired.
   B. Master keys should have no markings that will identify them as such and the list of holders of these keys should be frequently reviewed to determine the continuing necessity for the individuals having them.
   C. Whenever keys for outside doors or gates or for other doors which permit access to important buildings and areas are misplaced, the locks should be immediately changed or replaced pending an investigation.
   D. Whenever an employee fails to return a borrowed key at the time specified, a prompt investigation should be made by the security force.

9. In a crowded building, a fire develops in the basement, and smoke enters the crowded rooms on the first floor. Of the following, the BEST action for an officer to take after an alarm is turned in is to

   A. call out a warning that the building is on fire and that everyone should evacuate because of the immediate danger
   B. call all of the officers together for an emergency meeting and discuss a plan of action
   C. immediately call for assistance from the local police station to help in evacuating the crowd
   D. tell everyone that there is a fire in the building next door and that they should move out onto the streets through available exits

10. Which of the following is in a key position to carry out successfully a safety program of an agency? The

    A. building engineer
    B. bureau chiefs
    C. immediate supervisors
    D. public relations director

11. It is GENERALLY considered that a daily roll call inspection, which checks to see that the officers and their equipment are in good order, is   11.____

    A. *desirable,* chiefly because it informs the superior officer what men will have to purchase new uniforms within a month
    B. *desirable,* chiefly because the public forms their impressions of the organization from the appearance of the officers
    C. *undesirable,* chiefly because this kind of daily inspection unnecessarily delays officers in getting to their assigned patrol posts
    D. *undesirable,* chiefly because roll call inspection usually misses individuals reporting to work late

12. A supervising officer in giving instructions to a group of officers on the principles of accident investigation remarked, "A conclusion that appears reasonable will often be changed by exploring a factor of apparently little importance".   12.____
    Which one of the following precautions does this statement emphasize as MOST important in any accident investigation?

    A. Every accident clue should be fully investigated.
    B. Accidents should not be too promptly investigated.
    C. Only specially trained officers should investigate accidents.
    D. Conclusions about accident causes are highly unreliable.

13. On a rainy day, a senior officer found that 9 of his 50 officers reported to work. What percentage of his officers was ABSENT?   13.____

    A. 18%   B. 80%   C. 82%   D. 90%

14. Officer A and Officer B work at the same post on the same days, but their hours are different. Officer A comes to work at 9:00 A.M. and leaves at 5:00 P.M., with a lunch period between 12:15 P.M. and 1:15 P.M. Officer B comes to work at 10:50 A.M. and works until 6:50 P.M., and he takes an hour for lunch between 3:00 P.M. and 4:00 P.M. What is the total amount of time between 9:00 A.M. and 6:50 P.M. that only ONE officer will be on duty?   14.____

    A. 4 hours   B. 4 hours and 40 minutes
    C. 5 hours   D. 5 hours and 40 minutes

15. An officer's log recorded the following attendance of 30 officers: 15.____
    Monday   20   present;   10   absent
    Tuesday   28   present;   2   absent
    Wednesday   30   present;   0   absent
    Thursday   21   present;   9   absent
    Friday   16   present;   14   absent
    Saturday   11   present;   19   absent
    Sunday   14   present;   16   absent
    On the average, how many men were present on the weekdays (Monday - Friday)?

    A. 21   B. 23   C. 25   D. 27

16. An angry woman is being questioned by an officer when she begins shouting abuses at him.
The BEST of the following procedures for the officer to follow is to

   A. leave the room until she has cooled off
   B. politely ignore anything she says
   C. place her under arrest by handcuffing her to a fixed object
   D. warn her that he will have to use force to restrain her making remarks

17. Of the following, which is NOT a recommended practice for an officer placing a woman offender under arrest?

   A. Assume that the offender is an innocent and virtuous person and treat her accordingly.
   B. Protect himself from attack by the woman.
   C. Refrain from using excessive physical force on the offender.
   D. Make the public aware that he is not abusing the woman.

Questions 18-21.

DIRECTIONS: Questions 18 through 21 are to be answered SOLELY on the basis of the following passage.

Specific measures for prevention of pilferage will be based on careful analysis of the conditions at each agency. The most practical and effective method to control casual pilferage is the establishment of psychological deterrents.

One of the most common means of discouraging casual pilferage is to search individuals leaving the agency at unannounced times and places. These spot searches may occasionally detect attempts at theft but greater value is realized by bringing to the attention of individuals the fact that they may be apprehended if they do attempt the illegal removal of property.

An aggressive security education program is an effective means of convincing employees that they have much more to lose than they do to gain by engaging in acts of theft. It is important for all employees to realize that pilferage is morally wrong no matter how insignificant the value of the item which is taken. In establishing any deterrent to casual pilferage, security officers must not lose sight of the fact that most employees are honest and disapprove of thievery. Mutual respect between security personnel and other employees of the agency must be maintained if the facility is to be protected from other more dangerous forms of human hazards. Any security measure which infringes on the human rights or dignity of others will jeopardize, rather than enhance, the overall protection of the agency.

18. The $100,000 yearly inventory of an agency revealed that $50 worth of goods had been stolen; the only individuals with access to the stolen materials were the employees. Of the following measures, which would the author of the preceding paragraph MOST likely recommend to a security officer?

   A. Conduct an intensive investigation of all employees to find the culprit.
   B. Make a record of the theft, but take no investigative or disciplinary action against any employee.
   C. Place a tight security check on all future movements of personnel.
   D. Remove the remainder of the material to an area with much greater security.

19. What does the passage imply is the percentage of employees whom a security officer should expect to be honest?

    A. No employee can be expected to be honest all of the time
    B. Just 50%
    C. Less than 50%
    D. More than 50%

20. According to the passage, the security officer would use which of the following methods to minimize theft in buildings with many exits when his staff is very small?

    A. Conduct an inventory of all material and place a guard near that which is most likely to be pilfered.
    B. Inform employees of the consequences of legal prosecution for pilfering.
    C. Close off the unimportant exits and have all his men concentrate on a few exits.
    D. Place a guard at each exit and conduct a casual search of individuals leaving the premises.

21. Of the following, the title BEST suited for this passage is:

    A. Control Measures for Casual Pilfering
    B. Detecting the Potential Pilferer
    C. Financial losses Resulting from Pilfering
    D. The Use of Moral Persuasion in Physical Security

22. Of the following first aid procedures, which will cause the GREATEST harm in treating a fracture?

    A. Control hemorrhages by applying direct pressure
    B. Keep the broken portion from moving about
    C. Reset a protruding bone by pressing it back into place
    D. Treat the suffering person for shock

23. During a snowstorm, a man comes to you complaining of frostbitten hands.
    PROPER first aid treatment in this case is to

    A. place the hands under hot running water
    B. place the hands in lukewarm water
    C. call a hospital and wait for medical aid
    D. rub the hands in melting snow

24. While on duty, an officer sees a woman apparently in a state of shock.
    Of the following, which one is NOT a symptom of shock?

    A. Eyes lacking luster
    B. A cold, moist forehead
    C. A shallow, irregular breathing
    D. A strong, throbbing pulse

25. You notice a man entering your building who begins coughing violently, has shortness of breath, and complains of severe chest pains.
    These symptoms are GENERALLY indicative of

    A. a heart attack
    B. a stroke
    C. internal bleeding
    D. an epileptic seizure

26. When an officer is required to record the rolled fingerprint impressions of a prisoner on the standard fingerprint form, the technique recommended by the F.B.I, as MOST likely to result in obtaining clear impressions is to roll

   A. all fingers away from the center of the prisoner's body
   B. all fingers toward the center of the prisoner's body
   C. the thumbs away from and the other fingers toward the center of the prisoner's body
   D. the thumbs toward and the other fingers away from the center of the prisoner's body

27. The principle which underlies the operation and use of a lie detector machine is that

   A. a person who is not telling the truth will be able to give a consistent story
   B. a guilty mind will unconsciously associate ideas in a very indicative manner
   C. the presence of emotional stress in a person will result in certain abnormal physical reactions
   D. many individuals are not afraid to lie

Questions 28-32.

DIRECTIONS: Questions 28 through 32 are based SOLELY on the following diagram and the paragraph preceding this group of questions. The paragraph will be divided into two statements. Statement one (1) consists of information given to the senior officer by an agency director; *this information will detail the specific security objectives the senior officer has to meet.* Statement two (2) gives the resources available to the senior officer.

NOTE: The questions are correctly answered only when all of the agency's objectives have been met and when the officer has used all his resources efficiently (i.e., to their maximum effectiveness) in meeting these objectives. All X's in the diagram indicate possible locations of officers' posts. Each X has a corresponding number which is to be used when referring to that location.

DIAGRAM

Main entrance

→ Door
x .... Post Location

[Floor plan diagram showing:
- Room G (upper left) with posts x5, x4, x3; Door T, Door S
- Post x7 near Door A
- Room F (upper area) with post x8 near Door C (stairway)
- Lavatory (center) with Door R, posts x9, x10
- Room H (lower middle) with post x11, x1; Door D
- Lavatory (lower left) with Door Q, post x2
- Stairway (bottom center)
- Door P, posts x12, x13
- Room J — office for Authorized Personnel (lower right)]

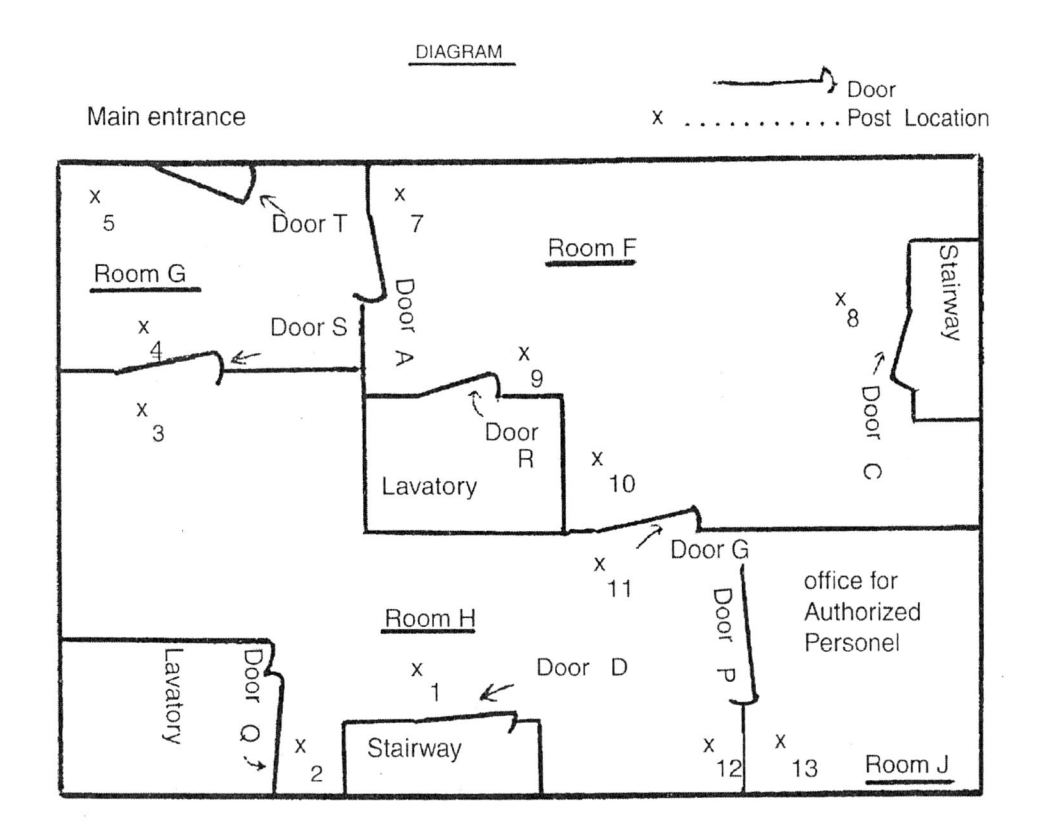

PARAGRAPH

PARAGRAPH

STATEMENT 1: Room G will be the public intake room from which persons will be directed to Room F or Room H; under no circumstances are they to enter the wrong room, and they are not to move from Room F to Room H or vice-versa. A minimum of two officers must be in each room frequented by the public at all times, and they are to keep unauthorized individuals from going to the second floor or into restricted areas. All usable entrances or exits must be covered.

STATEMENT 2: The senior officer can lock any door except the main entrance and stairway doors. He has a staff of five officers to carry out these operations.

NOTE: The senior officer is available for guard duty. Room J is an active office.

28. According to the instructions, how many officers should be assigned inside the office for authorized personnel (Room J)?   28._____

    A. 0   B. 1   C. 2   D. 3

29. In order to keep the public from moving between Room F and Room H, which door(s) can be locked without interfering with normal office operations? Door   29._____

    A. G   B. P   C. R and Q   D. S

30. When placing officers in Room H, the only way the senior officer can satisfy the agency's objectives and his manpower limitations is by placing men at locations 30.____

    A. 1 and 3   B. 1 and 12   C. 3 and 11   D. 11 and 12

31. In accordance with the instructions, the LEAST effective locations to place officers in Room F are locations 31.____

    A. 7 and 9   B. 7 and 10   C. 8 and 9   D. 9 and 10

32. In which room is it MOST difficult for each of the officers to see all the movements of the public? Room 32.____

    A. G   B. F   C. H   D. J

33. According to its own provisions, the Penal Law of the State has a number of general purposes. 33.____
    It would be LEAST accurate to state that one of these general purposes is to

    A. give fair warning of the nature of the conduct forbidden and the penalties authorized upon conviction
    B. define the act or omission and accompanying mental state which constitute each offense
    C. regulate the procedure which governs the arrest, trial and punishment of convicted offenders
    D. insure the public safety by preventing the commission of offenses through the deterrent influence of the sentences authorized upon conviction

34. Officers must be well-informed about the meaning of certain terms in connection with their enforcement duties. Which one of the following statements about such terms would be MOST accurate according to the Penal Law of the State? A(n) 34.____

    A. offense is always a crime
    B. offense is always a violation
    C. violation is never a crime
    D. felony is never an offense

35. According to the Penal Law of the State, the one of the following elements which must ALWAYS be present in order to justify the arrest of a person for criminal assault is 35.____

    A. the infliction of an actual physical injury
    B. an intent to cause an injury
    C. a threat to inflict a physical injury
    D. the use of some kind of weapon

36. A recent law of the State defines who are police officers and who are peace officers. The official title of this law is: The 36.____

    A. Criminal Code of Procedure
    B. Law of Criminal Procedure
    C. Criminal Procedure Law
    D. Code of Criminal Procedure

37. If you are required to appear in court to testify as the complainant in a criminal action, it would be MOST important for you to

   A. confine your answers to the questions asked when you are testifying
   B. help the prosecutor even if some exaggeration in your testimony may be necessary
   C. be as fair as possible to the defendant even if some details have to be omitted from your testimony
   D. avoid contradicting other witnesses testifying against the defendant

38. A senior officer is asked by the television news media to explain to the public what happened on his post during an important incident.
When speaking with departmental permission in front of the tape recorders and cameras, the senior officer can give the MOST favorable impression of himself and his department by

   A. refusing to answer any questions but remaining calm in front of the cameras
   B. giving a detailed report of the wrong decisions made by his agency for handling the particular incident
   C. presenting the appropriate factual information in a competent way
   D. telling what should have been done during the incident and how such incidents will be handled in the future

39. Of the following suggested guidelines for officers, the one which is LEAST likely to be effective in promoting good manners and courtesy in their daily contacts with the public is:

   A. Treat inquiries by telephone in the same manner as those made in person
   B. Never look into the face of the person to whom you are speaking
   C. Never give misinformation in answer to any inquiry on a matter on which you are uncertain of the facts
   D. Show respect and consideration in both trivial and important contacts with the public

40. Assume you are an officer who has had a record of submitting late weekly reports and that you are given an order by your supervisor which is addressed to all line officers. The order states that weekly reports will be replaced by twice-weekly reports.
The MOST logical conclusion for you to make, of the following, is:

   A. Fully detailed information was missing from your past reports
   B. Most officers have submitted late reports
   C. The supervisor needs more timely information
   D. The supervisor is attempting to punish you for your past late reports

41. A young man with long hair and "mod" clothing makes a complaint to an officer about the rudeness of another officer.
If the senior officer is not on the premises, the officer receiving the complaint should

   A. consult with the officer who is being accused to see if the youth's story is true
   B. refer the young man to central headquarters
   C. record the complaint made against his fellow officer and ask the youth to wait until he can locate the senior officer
   D. search for the senior officer and bring him back to the site of the complainant

42. During a demonstration, which area should ALWAYS be kept clear of demonstrators? 42.___

    A. Water fountains   B. Seating areas
    C. Doorways   D. Restrooms

43. During demonstrations, an officer's MOST important duty is to 43.___

    A. aid the agency's employees to perform their duties
    B. promptly arrest those who might cause incidents
    C. promptly disperse the crowds of demonstrators
    D. keep the demonstrators from disrupting order

44. Of the following, what is the FIRST action a senior officer should take if a demonstration develops in his area without advance warning? 44.___

    A. Call for additional assistance from the police department
    B. Find the leaders of the demonstrators and discuss their demands
    C. See if the demonstrators intend to break the law
    D. Inform his superiors of the event taking place

45. If a senior officer is informed in the morning that a demonstration will take place during the afternoon at his assigned location, he should assemble his officers to discuss the nature and aspects of this demonstration. Of the following, the subject which it is LEAST important to discuss during this meeting is 45.___

    A. making a good impression if an officer is called before the television cameras for a personal interview
    B. the known facts and causes of the demonstration
    C. the attitude and expected behavior of the demonstrators
    D. the individual responsibilities of the officers during the demonstration

46. A male officer has probable reason to believe that a group of women occupying the ladies' toilet are using illicit drugs.
    The BEST action, of the following, for the officer to take is to 46.___

    A. call for assistance and, with the aid of such assistance, enter the toilet and escort the occupants outside
    B. ignore the situation but recommend that the ladies' toilet be closed temporarily
    C. immediately rush into the ladies' toilet and search the occupants therein
    D. knock on the door of the ladies' toilet and ask their permission to enter so that he will not be accused of trying to molest them

47. Assume that you know that a group of demonstrators will not cooperate with your request to throw handbills in a waste basket instead of on the sidewalk. You ask one of the leaders of the group, who agrees with you, to speak to the demonstrators and ask for their cooperation in this matter.
    Your request of the group leader is 47.___

    A. *desirable,* chiefly because an officer needs civilians to control the public since the officer is usually unfriendly to the views of public groups
    B. *undesirable,* chiefly because an officer should never request a civilian to perform his duties
    C. *desirable,* chiefly because the appeal of an acknowledged leader helps in gaining group cooperation

D. *undesirable,* chiefly because an institutional leader is motivated to maneuver a situation to gain his own personal advantage

48. A vague letter received from a female employee in the agency accuses an officer of improper conduct.
The initial investigative interview by the senior officer assigned to check the accusation should GENERALLY be with the

   A. accused officer
   B. female employee
   C. highest superior about disciplinary action against the officer
   D. immediate supervisor of the female employee

Questions 49-50.

DIRECTIONS: Questions 49 and 50 are to be answered SOLELY on the basis of the information in the following paragraph.

The personal conduct of each member of the Department is the primary factor in promoting desirable police-community relations. Tact, patience, and courtesy shall be strictly observed under all circumstances. A favorable public attitude toward the police must be earned; it is influenced by the personal conduct and attitude of each member of the force, by his personal integrity and courteous manner, by his respect for due process of law, by his devotion to the principles of justice, fairness, and impartiality.

49. According to the preceding paragraph, what is the BEST action an officer can take in dealing with people in a neighborhood?

   A. Assist neighborhood residents by doing favors for them.
   B. Give special attention to the community leaders in order to be able to control them effectively.
   C. Behave in an appropriate manner and give all community members the same just treatment.
   D. Prepare a plan detailing what he, the officer, wants to do for the community and submit it for approval.

50. As used in the paragraph, the word *impartiality* means *most nearly*

   A. observant   B. unbiased
   C. righteousness   D. honesty

KEY (CORRECT ANSWERS)

1. B	11. B	21. A	31. D	41. C
2. B	12. A	22. C	32. C	42. C
3. A	13. C	23. B	33. C	43. D
4. A	14. D	24. D	34. C	44. D
5. D	15. B	25. A	35. A	45. A
6. C	16. B	26. D	36. C	46. A
7. D	17. A	27. C	37. A	47. C
8. C	18. B	28. A	38. C	48. B
9. D	19. D	29. A	39. B	49. C
10. C	20. B	30. B	40. C	50. B

TEST 2

DIRECTIONS: Each question or incomplete statement is followed by several suggested answers or completions. Select the one that BEST answers the question or completes the statement. *PRINT THE LETTER OF THE CORRECT ANSWER IN THE SPACE AT THE RIGHT.*

Questions 1-5.

DIRECTIONS: Questions 1 through 5 consist of short paragraphs. Each paragraph contains one word which is INCORRECTLY used because it is NOT in keeping with the meaning of the paragraph. Find the word in each paragraph which is INCORRECTLY used, and then select as the answer the suggested word which should be substituted for the incorrectly used word.

SAMPLE QUESTION

In determining who is to do the work in your unit, you will have to decide just who does what from day to day. One of your lowest responsibilities is to assign work so that everybody gets a fair share and that everyone can do his part well.
    A. new   B. old   C. important   D. performance

EXPLANATION

The word which is NOT in keeping with the meaning of the paragraph is "lowest". This is the INCORRECTLY used word. The suggested word "important" would be in keeping with the meaning of the paragraph and should be substituted for "lowest". Therefore, the CORRECT answer is Choice C.

1. If really good practice in the elimination of preventable injuries is to be achieved and held in any establishment, top management must refuse full and definite responsibility and must apply a good share of its attention to the task.

    A. accept   B. avoidable   C. duties   D. problem

2. Recording the human face for identification is by no means the only service performed by the camera in the field of investigation. When the trial of any issue takes place, a word picture is sought to be distorted to the court of incidents, occurrences, or events which are in dispute.

    A. appeals   B. description
    C. portrayed   D. deranged

3. In the collection of physical evidence, it cannot be emphasized too strongly that a haphazard systematic search at the scene of the crime is vital. Nothing must be overlooked. Often the only leads in a case will come from the results of this search.

    A. important   B. investigation
    C. proof   D. thorough

4. If an investigator has reason to suspect that the witness is mentally stable or a habitual drunkard, he should leave no stone unturned in his investigation to determine if the witness was under the influence of liquor or drugs, or was mentally unbalanced either at the time of the occurrence to which he testified or at the time of the trial.

    A. accused   B. clue   C. deranged   D. question

1.____

2.____

3.____

4.____

5. The use of records is a valuable step in crime investigation and is the main reason every department should maintain accurate reports. Crimes are not committed through the use of departmental records alone but from the use of all records, of almost every type, wherever they may be found and whenever they give any incidental information regarding the criminal.

    A. accidental   B. necessary   C. reported   D. solved

Questions 6-8.

DIRECTIONS: Questions 6 through 8 are to be answered SOLELY on the basis of the following passage.

The mass media are an integral part of the daily life of virtually every American. Among these media, the youngest, television, is the most persuasive. Ninety-five percent of American homes have at least one television set, and on the average that set is in use for about 40 hours each week. The central place of television in American life makes this medium the focal point of a growing national concern over the effects of media portrayals of violence on the values, attitudes, and behavior of an ever increasing audience.

In our concern about violence and its causes, it is easy to make television a scapegoat. But we emphasise the fact that there is no simple answer to the problem of violence -- no single explanation of its causes, and no single prescription for its control. It should be remembered that America also experienced high levels of crime and violence in periods before the advent of television.

The problem of balance, taste, and artistic merit in entertaining programs on television are complex. We cannot countenance government censorship of television. Nor would we seek to impose arbitrary limitations on programming which might jeopardize television's ability to deal in dramatic presentations with controversial social issues. Nonetheless, we are deeply troubled by television's constant portrayal of violence, not in any genuine attempt to focus artistic expression on the human condition, but rather in pandering to a public preoccupation with violence that television itself has helped to generate.

6. According to the passage, television uses violence MAINLY

    A. to highlight the reality of everyday existence
    B. to satisfy the audience's hunger for destructive action
    C. to shape the values and attitudes of the public
    D. when it films documentaries concerning human conflict

7. Which one of the following statements is BEST supported by this passage?

    A. Early American history reveals a crime pattern which is not related to television.
    B. Programs should give presentations of social issues and never portray violent acts.
    C. Television has proven that entertainment programs can easily make the balance between taste and artistic merit a simple matter.
    D. Values and behavior should be regulated by governmental censorship.

8. Of the following, which word has the same meaning as countenance as it is used in the above passage?

    A. approve   B. exhibit   C. oppose   D. reject

Questions 9-12.

DIRECTIONS: Questions 9 through 12 are to be answered SOLELY on the basis of the following graph relating to the burglary rate in the city, 2003 to 2008, inclusive.

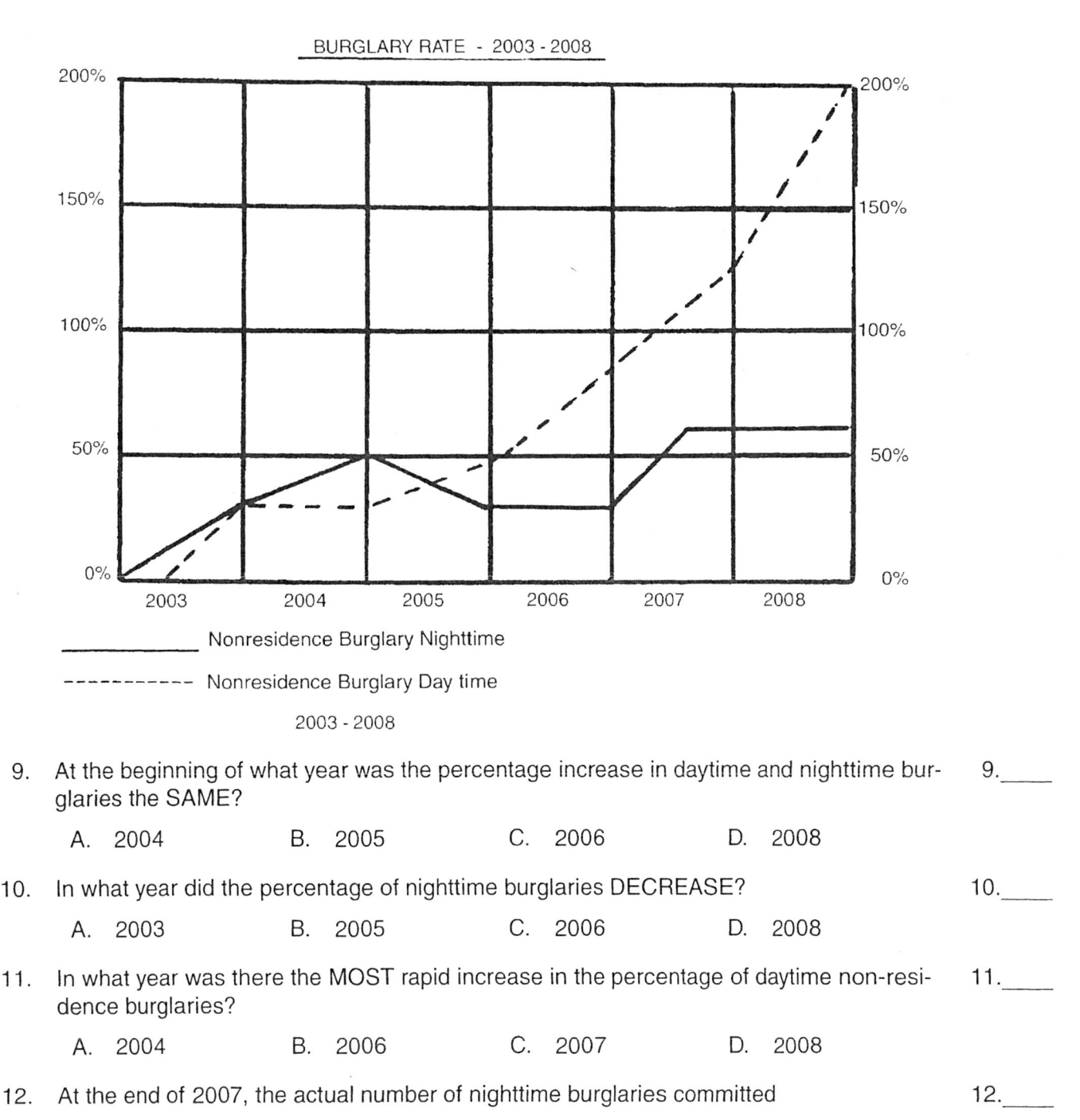

BURGLARY RATE - 2003 - 2008

——————— Nonresidence Burglary Nighttime

- - - - - - - - - - Nonresidence Burglary Day time

2003 - 2008

9. At the beginning of what year was the percentage increase in daytime and nighttime burglaries the SAME? 9.____

    A. 2004   B. 2005   C. 2006   D. 2008

10. In what year did the percentage of nighttime burglaries DECREASE? 10.____

    A. 2003   B. 2005   C. 2006   D. 2008

11. In what year was there the MOST rapid increase in the percentage of daytime non-residence burglaries? 11.____

    A. 2004   B. 2006   C. 2007   D. 2008

12. At the end of 2007, the actual number of nighttime burglaries committed 12.____

    A. was about 20%
    B. was 40%
    C. was 400
    D. cannot be determined from the information given

Questions 13-17.

DIRECTIONS: Questions 13 through 17 consist of two sentences numbered 1 and 2 taken from police officers' reports. Some of these sentences are correct according to ordinary formal English usage. Other sentences are incorrect because they contain errors in English usage or punctuation. Consider a sentence correct if it contains no errors in English usage or punctuation even if there may be other ways of writing the sentence correctly. Mark your answer to each question in the space at the right as follows:
  A. If only sentence 1 is correct, but not sentence 2
  B. If only sentence 2 is correct, but not sentence 1
  C. If sentences 1 and 2 are both correct
  D. If sentences 1 and 2 are both incorrect

SAMPLE QUESTION
  1. The woman claimed that the purse was her's.
  2. Everyone of the new officers was assigned to a patrol post.

EXPLANATION

Sentence 1 is INCORRECT because of an error in punctuation. The possessive words, "ours, yours, hers, theirs," do not have the apostrophe (').

Sentence 2 is CORRECT because the subject of the sentence is "Everyone" which is singular and requires the singular verb "was assigned".

Since only sentence 2 is correct, but not sentence 1, the CORRECT answer is B.

13. 1. Either the patrolman or his sergeant are always ready to help the public.   13.___
    2. The sergeant asked the patrolman when he would finish the report.

14. 1. The injured man could not hardly talk.   14.___
    2. Every officer had ought to hand in their reports on time.

15. 1. Approaching the victim of the assault, two large bruises were noticed by me.   15.___
    2. The prisoner was arrested for assault, resisting arrest, and use of a deadly weapon.

16. 1. A copy of the orders, which had been prepared by the captain, was given to each patrolman.   16.___
    2. It's always necessary to inform an arrested person of his constitutional rights before asking him any questions.

17. 1. To prevent further bleeding, I applied a tourniquet tothe wound.   17.___
    2. John Rano a senior officer was on duty at the time of the accident.

Questions 18-25.

DIRECTIONS: Answer each of Questions 18 through 25 SOLELY on the basis of the statement preceding the questions.

18. The criminal is one whose habits have been erroneously developed or, we should say, developed in anti-social patterns, and therefore the task of dealing with him is not one of punishment, but of treatment.   18.___
    The basic principle expressed in this statement is BEST illustrated by the

    A. emphasis upon rehabilitation in penal institutions
    B. prevalence of capital punishment for murder
    C. practice of imposing heavy fines for minor violations
    D. legal provision for trial by jury in criminal cases

19. The writ of habeas corpus is one of the great guarantees of personal liberty. Of the following, the BEST justification for this statement is that the writ of habeas corpus is frequently used to

    A. compel the appearance in court of witnesses who are outside the state
    B. obtain the production of books and records at a criminal trial
    C. secure the release of a person improperly held in custody
    D. prevent the use of deception in obtaining testimony of reluctant witnesses

20. Fifteen persons suffered effects of carbon dioxide asphyxiation shortly before noon recently in a seventh-floor pressing shop. The accident occurred in a closed room where six steam presses were in operation. Four men and one woman were overcome.
    Of the following, the MOST probable reason for the fact that so many people were affected simultaneously is that

    A. women evidently show more resistance to the effects of carbon dioxide than men
    B. carbon dioxide is an odorless and colorless gas
    C. carbon dioxide is lighter than air
    D. carbon dioxide works more quickly at higher altitudes

21. Lay the patient on his stomach, one arm extended directly overhead, the other arm bent at the elbow, and with the face turned outward and resting on hand or forearm.
    To the officer who is skilled at administering first aid, these instructions should IMMEDIATELY suggest

    A. application of artificial respiration
    B. treatment for third degree burns of the arm
    C. setting a dislocated shoulder
    D. control of capillary bleeding in the stomach

22. The soda and acid fire extinguisher is the hand extinguisher most commonly used by officers. The main body of the cylinder is filled with a mixture of water and bicarbonate of soda. In a separate interior compartment, at the top, is a small bottle of sulphuric acid. When the extinguisher is inverted, the acid spills into the solution below and starts a chemical reaction. The carbon dioxide thereby generated forces the solution from the extinguisher.
    The officer who understands the operation of this fire extinguisher should know that it is LEAST likely to operate properly

    A. in basements or cellars
    B. in extremely cold weather
    C. when the reaction is of a chemical nature
    D. when the bicarbonate of soda is in solution

23. Suppose that, at a training lecture, you are told that many of the men in our penal institutions today are second and third offenders.
    Of the following, the MOST valid inference you can make SOLELY on the basis of this statement is that

    A. second offenders are not easily apprehended
    B. patterns of human behavior are not easily changed
    C. modern laws are not sufficiently flexible
    D. laws do not breed crimes

24. In all societies of our level of culture, acts are committed which arouse censure severe enough to take the form of punishment by the government. Such acts are crimes, not because of their inherent nature, but because of their ability to arouse resentment and to stimulate repressive measures.
Of the following, the MOST valid inference which can be drawn from this statement is that

   A. society unjustly punishes acts which are inherently criminal
   B. many acts are not crimes but are punished by society because such acts threaten the lives of innocent people
   C. only modern society has a level of culture
   D. societies sometimes disagree as to what acts are crimes

25. Crime cannot be measured directly. Its amount must be inferred from the frequency of some occurrence connected with it; for example, crimes brought to the attention of the police, persons arrested, prosecutions, convictions, and other dispositions, such as probation or commitment. Each of these may be used as an index of the amount of crime.
SOLELY on the basis of the foregoing statement, it is MOST correct to state that

   A. the incidence of crime cannot be estimated with any accuracy
   B. the number of commitments is usually greater than the number of probationary sentences
   C. the amount of crime is ordinarily directly correlated with the number of persons arrested
   D. a joint consideration of crimes brought to the attention of the police and the number of prosecutions undertaken gives little indication of the amount of crime in a locality

KEY (CORRECT ANSWERS)

1.	B		11.	D
2.	A		12.	D
3.	D		13.	D
4.	C		14.	D
5.	D		15.	B
6.	B		16.	C
7.	A		17.	A
8.	A		18.	A
9.	A		19.	C
10.	B		20.	B

21. A
22. B
23. B
24. D
25. C

EXAMINATION SECTION
TEST 1

DIRECTIONS: Each question or incomplete statement is followed by several suggested answers or completions. Select the one that BEST answers the question or completes the statement. *PRINT THE LETTER OF THE CORRECT ANSWER IN THE SPACE AT THE RIGHT.*

Questions 1-9.

DIRECTIONS: Questions 1 through 9 are to be answered SOLELY on the basis of the following information and the DIRECTORY OF SERVICES.

Officer Johnson has just been assigned to the North End Service Facility and is now on his post in the main lobby. The facility is open to the public from 9 A.M. to 5 P.M. each Monday through Friday, except on Thursdays when it is open from 9 A.M. to 7 P.M. The facility is closed on holidays.

Officer Johnson must ensure an orderly flow of visitors through the lobby of the facility. To accomplish this, Officer Johnson gives directions and provides routine information to clients and other members of the public who enter and leave the facility through the lobby.

In order to give directions and provide routine information to visitors, such as information concerning the location of services, Officer Johnson consults the Directory of Services shown below. Officer Johnson must ensure that clients are directed to the correct room for service and are sent to that room only during the hours that the particular service is available. When clients ask for the location of more than one service, they should be directed to go first to the service that will close soonest.

NORTH END SERVICE FACILITY
DIRECTORY OF SERVICES

Room	Type of Service	Days Available	Hours Open
101	Facility Receptionist	Monday, Tuesday, Wednesday, Friday	9 AM- 5 PM
		Thursday	9 AM- 7 PM
103	Photo Identification Cards	Monday, Wednesday, Friday	9 AM-12 Noon
104	Lost and Stolen Identification Cards	Wednesday, Thursday	9 AM-5 PM
105	Applications for Welfare/Food Stamps	Wednesday, Friday	1 PM-5 PM
107	Recertification for Welfare/Food Stamps	Monday, Thursday	10 AM- 12 Noon
108	Medicaid Applications	Tuesday, Wednesday	2 PM-5 PM
109	Medicaid Complaints	Tuesday, Wednesday	10 AM-2 PM
110, 111	Social Worker	Monday, Wednesday Tuesday, Friday Thursday	9 AM-12 Noon 1 PM-5 PM 9 AM- 5 PM
114	Hearing Room (By appointment only)	Monday, Thursday	9 AM-5 PM

DIRECTORY OF SERVICES
(CONT'D)

Room	Type of Service	Days Available	Hours Open
115	Hearing Information	Monday, Tuesday, Wednesday, Thursday, Friday	9 AM-1 PM
206, 207	Nutrition Aid	Monday, Wednesday, Friday Tuesday, Thursday	10 AM-2 PM 9 AM-12 Noon
215	Health Clinic	Monday, Tuesday, Wednesday, Friday Thursday	9 AM-5 PM 9 AM-7 PM
220	Facility Administrative Office	Monday, Tuesday, Wednesday, Thursday, Friday	9 AM-5 PM

1. It is Tuesday morning and Ms. Loretta Rogers, a client of the North End Service Facility, asks Officer Johnson where she should go in order to apply for Medicaid. Officer Johnson tells Ms. Rogers to go to Room _____ at _____.

   A. 108; 1:00 P.M.
   B. 109; 11:00 A.M.
   C. 108; 2:00 P.M.
   D. 109; 2:00 P.M.

2. On Friday at 11:00 A.M., Mrs. Ruth Ramos, a new client at the North End Service Facility, tells Officer Johnson that she wants to obtain a photo identification card and see a social worker.
   Officer Johnson should direct Mrs. Ramos to first go to Room

   A. 103   B. 104   C. 110   D. 220

3. On Friday at 10:30 A.M., a client at the North End Service Facility who is directed by Officer Johnson to go to Room 206 will be able to receive service regarding

   A. Recertification for Welfare/Food Stamps
   B. Hearing Information
   C. Medicaid Applications
   D. Nutrition Aid

4. At 9:00 A.M. on Monday, a client at the North End Service Facility who is directed by Officer Johnson to Room 101 for service will find

   A. Nutrition Aid
   B. Facility Receptionist
   C. Health Clinic
   D. Hearing Information

5. On Tuesday at 12:30 P.M., Mr. Paul Brown tells Officer Johnson that he lost his identification card and wants to obtain a new one as soon as possible.
   Officer Johnson should direct Mr. Brown to go to Room 104

   A. immediately
   B. at 1:00 P.M. that day
   C. at 9:00 A.M. on Wednesday
   D. at 2:00 P.M. on Friday

6. A client at the North End Service Facility explains to Officer Johnson that he wants to make an appointment with a Social Worker.
   The client should be directed to go to Room

   A. 104   B. 110   C. 115   D. 215

7. Ms. Alice Lee is a client at the North End Service Facility who has a 10:00 A.M. appointment on Thursday in the Hearing Room and does not know where to go.
   Officer Johnson should direct Ms. Lee to go to Room

   A. 101   B. 110   C. 112   D. 114

8. Officer Johnson is asked by a visitor which services are available on Thursdays between 5:00 P.M. and 7:00 P.M. Officer Johnson should inform the visitor that an available service during that time is

   A. Health Clinic   B. Medicaid Complaints
   C. Nutrition Aid   D. Social Worker

9. Mr. Jack Klein, a visitor to the North End Service Facility, asks Officer Johnson when and where he can file a complaint concerning Medicaid.
   Officer Johnson should inform Mr. Klein that he may go to Room

   A. 108 on Tuesday or Wednesday between 2:00 P.M. and 5:00 P.M.
   B. 109 on Tuesday or Wednesday between 10:00 A.M. and 2:00 P.M.
   C. 115 on Monday or Tuesday between 10:00 A.M. and 12:00 Noon
   D. 215 on Thursday between 9:00 A.M. and 7:00 P.M.

Questions 10-12.

DIRECTIONS: Questions 10 through 12 are to be answered SOLELY on the basis of the following information.

Security Officers should act in accordance with guidelines included in a manual provided to security staff. Assume that the following guidelines apply to Officers when in contact with visitors or clients in a facility:

1. Try to see things from the visitor's or client's point of view.
2. Ignore insulting comments.
3. Maintain a calm and patient manner.
4. Speak quietly, courteously, and tactfully.

10. Officer Renee Williams is patrolling the lobby area of her facility when she hears a client angrily yelling at the receptionist. She goes to investigate the situation and finds out from the receptionist that the client is one hour late for his appointment with a social worker who now has other appointments. The client demands to be seen by the social worker immediately. Officer Williams angrily tells the client that it is his own fault that he missed his appointment and he should stop bothering the receptionist and go home.
    In this situation, Officer Williams' behavior towards the client is

    A. *proper,* chiefly because it is the client's fault that he missed his appointment
    B. *improper,* chiefly because security officers should stay calm and speak courteously when dealing with clients
    C. *proper,* chiefly because the client had yelled at the receptionist
    D. *improper,* chiefly because the security officer should have ignored the whole incident

11. During his tour, Officer Montgomery is passing through his facility's waiting room on the way to the cafeteria for a break. As Officer Montgomery passes by a visitor, the visitor mutters an insulting remark about the Officer's appearance. Officer Montgomery ignores the visitor and the remark and proceeds on his way to the cafeteria.
Officer Montgomery's action in this situation is

   A. *correct,* chiefly because it is not necessary for Officer Montgomery to respond to visitors while on a break
   B. *incorrect,* chiefly because Officer Montgomery should have ejected the visitor from the facility
   C. *correct,* chiefly because special officers should ignore insults
   D. *incorrect,* chiefly because visitors should not be allowed to ridicule authority figures such as special officers

12. While patrolling the facility parking lot, Officer Klausner sees an unoccupied car parked in front of a fire hydrant. Officer Klausner writes out a summons for a parking violation and places it on the windshield of the car. As the Officer begins to walk away, the owner of the car spots the summons on the windshield and runs over to the car. The car owner is furious at getting the summons, confronts the Officer, and curses him loudly.
In this situation, Officer Klausner should

   A. curse back at the car owner just as loudly
   B. push him out of the way and resume patrol
   C. calmly explain to him the nature of the violation
   D. return all the insults but in a calm tone

Question 13.

DIRECTIONS: Question 13 is to be answered SOLELY on the basis of the following information.

Special Officers are permitted to give only general information about social services. They shall not provide advice concerning specific procedures.

13. Special Officer Lynn King is on post near the Medicaid Office in the Manhattan Income Maintenance Center. While Officer King is on post, a client approaches her and asks which forms must be filled out in order to apply for Medicaid benefits. Officer King tells the client that she cannot help him and directs the client to the Medicaid Office.
In this situation, Officer King's response to the client's question is

   A. *correct,* chiefly because Officer King's duties do not include providing any information to clients
   B. *incorrect,* chiefly because Officer King should have provided as much specific information as possible to the client
   C. *correct,* chiefly because Officer King may not advise clients on social services procedures
   D. *incorrect,* chiefly because Officer King should know which forms are used in the facility

Question 14.

DIRECTIONS: Question 14 is to be answered SOLELY on the basis of the following information.

Security Officers must request that visitors and clients show identification and inspect that identification before allowing them to enter restricted areas in the facility.

14. Security Officer Crane is assigned to a fixed post outside Commissioner Maxwell's office, which is a restricted area. A visitor approaches Officer Crane's desk and states that he is Robert Maxwell and has an appointment with the Commissioner, who is his brother. Officer Crane checks the appointment book, verifies that Robert Maxwell has an appointment with the Commissioner, and allows the visitor to enter the office.
In this situation, Officer Crane's action in allowing the visitor admittance to the Commissioner's office is

14.____

   A. *correct,* chiefly because he verified that Robert Maxwell had an appointment with the Commissioner
   B. *incorrect,* chiefly because all visitors must show identification before entering restricted areas
   C. *correct,* chiefly because it would insult the Commissioner's brother if he was asked to show identification
   D. *incorrect,* chiefly because he should have called the Commissioner to verify that he has a brother

Question 15.

DIRECTIONS: Question 15 is to be answered SOLELY on the basis of the following information.

While on duty, a Special Officer must give his rank, name, and shield number to any person who requests it.

15. Special Officer Karen Mitchell is assigned to patrol an area in the North Bronx Service Facility. While on patrol, Officer Mitchell observes a visitor asking other clients in the lobby for money. Upon investigation, she determines that the visitor has no official business in the facility and asks the visitor to leave the premises. The individual says that he will leave but demands to know Officer Mitchell's name and shield number.
In response to the visitor's demand, Officer Mitchell should

15.____

   A. give the individual her name and shield number
   B. inform him that he can only obtain that information from her supervisor
   C. ignore his demand and resume her patrol
   D. tell the visitor that she will issue a summons to him if he keeps bothering her

Question 16.

DIRECTIONS: Question 16 is to be answered SOLELY on the basis of the following information.

A member of the Security Staff must follow guidelines for providing information to reporters concerning official facility business. Special Officers shall not be interviewed, nor make public speeches or statements pertaining to official business unless authorized. Security Staff must receive authorization from the Office of Public Affairs before speaking to reporters on any matters pertaining to official facility business.

16. You are a Special Officer in a Men's Shelter. A reporter approaches you as you are leaving the building. The reporter requests that you give an insider's view on conditions in the shelter. He assures you that you will remain anonymous.
You should tell the reporter that you

- A. must obtain permission from your immediate supervisor before giving any interviews
- B. will be more than happy to provide him with information concerning conditions in the shelter
- C. must receive authorization from the Office of Public Affairs before giving any interviews
- D. may not give him any information, but that your supervisor will be able to provide him with the requested information.

Questions 17-21.

DIRECTIONS: Questions 17 through 21 are to be answered SOLELY on the basis of the following information.

During their tours, Security Officers are required to transmit and receive information and commands over two-way portable radios from other security staff members. Officers use a numbered code to transmit information over the radio. For example, an officer who calls *10-13* into his radio communicates to other officers and supervisors that he is in need of assistance. Assume that the code numbers shown below along with their specified meanings are those used by Special Officers.

Code	Meaning
10-01	Call your command
10-02	Report to your command
10-03	Call Dispatcher
10-04	Acknowledgment
10-05	Repeat message
10-06	Stand-by
10-07	Verify
10-08	Respond to specified area and advise
10-10	Investigate
10-13	Officer needs help
10-20	Robbery in progress
10-21	Burglary in progress
10-22	Larceny in progress
10-24	Assault in progress
10-30	Robbery has occurred

10-31	Burglary has occurred
10-34	Assault has occurred
10-40	Unusual incident
10-41	Vehicle accident
10-42	Traffic or parking problem
10-43	Electrical problem
10-50	Dispute or noise
10-52	Disorderly person/group
10-60	Ambulance needed
10-61	Police Department assistance required
10-64	Fire alarm
10-70	Arrived at scene
10-71	Arrest
10-72	Unfounded
10-73	Condition corrected
10-74	Resuming normal duties

17. Officer Cramer is patrolling Parking Lot A when he receives a radio message from Sergeant Wong. Sergeant Wong directs Officer Cramer to respond to Parking Lot B to investigate a reported traffic problem. Upon arriving at Parking Lot B, Officer Cramer observes a vehicle blocking a loading dock so that a delivery truck cannot gain access to the dock. After notification is made to the owner of the vehicle, the vehicle is moved, allowing the delivery truck to gain access to the loading dock. Which of the following should Officer Cramer use to BEST report the events that occurred back to Sergeant Wong?   17.____

    A. 10-72,10-41,10-73   B. 10-70,10-42,10-73
    C. 10-70, 10-41, 10-74   D. 10-72, 10-42,10-74

18. Officer Garret receives a message of *10-24, 10-10* on his radio from his supervisor, Sergeant Gomez. Officer Garret responds to the scene and later sends Sergeant Gomez the following message in response: *10-70, 10-72, 10-74*. Which of the following events are reported by use of those codes?   18.____
Sergeant Gomez ordered Officer Garret to investigate an assault

    A. in progress. Officer Garret arrived at the scene, discovered that the report was unfounded, and resumed normal duties.
    B. that had occurred. Officer Garret arrived at the scene, made an arrest, and then resumed normal duties.
    C. that had occurred. Officer Garret arrived at the scene and discovered that the report was unfounded and resumed normal duties.
    D. in progress. Officer Garret arrived at the scene, made an arrest, and then resumed normal duties.

19. Officer Torres is patrolling the grounds of his facility when he receives a radio message from Sergeant Washington. In response to the radio message, Officer Torres goes to the facility's parking lot and issues a summons to a vehicle blocking an ambulance entrance. The radio message that Officer Torres received from Sergeant Washington is 10-10,

   A. 10-21   B. 10-40   C. 10-42   D. 10-43

20. Officer Oxford transmits the following codes by radio to Sergeant Joseph: *10-20, 10-13*. The response that Officer Oxford receives from Sergeant Joseph on her radio is *10-04*. Which one of the following events are reported by the use of those codes?
    Officer Oxford informed Sergeant Joseph that

   A. a robbery was in progress and that she needs assistance, and Sergeant Joseph acknowledged her message
   B. an assault was in progress and that she wants him to respond to the area, and Sergeant Joseph acknowledged her message
   C. a burglary was in progress and that someone must investigate, and Sergeant Joseph responded that he is standing by
   D. a larceny was in progress and that she needs him to call a dispatcher. Sergeant Joseph reports this incident to his command.

21. While on patrol, Officer Robinson observes that the hall lights in Wing *B* are flickering on and off. Officer Robinson calls the Maintenance Office and a maintenance worker responds and corrects the problem.
    The radio code that Officer Robinson should transmit to his supervisor to report this incident is

   A. 10-06,10-08   B. 10-40,10-64
   C. 10-43,10-73   D. 10-61,10-07

Question 22.

DIRECTIONS: Question 22 is to be answered SOLELY on the basis of the following information.

The two-way portable radios used by Security or Special Officers to communicate with other security staff members are to be used for official business only. In addition, when transmitting official business, transmission time (time spent transmitting information to other staff) should be kept to a minimum.

22. During his tour, Special Officer Banks calls Sergeant Gates in the patrolroom over the radio and asks if his wife, Alice Banks, had telephoned. Sergeant Gates tells Officer Banks that his wife has not called. Officer Banks then requests that Sergeant Gates notify him as soon as his wife calls because he is expecting an important message concerning his family.
    In this situation, Officer Banks' use of his radio is

   A. *appropriate,* chiefly because his transmission time was not excessive
   B. *inappropriate,* chiefly because he should have made the transmission on his break
   C. *appropriate,* chiefly because his transmission concerned an important family matter
   D. *inappropriate,* chiefly because radios are to be used for official business only

Question 23.

DIRECTIONS: Question 23 is to be answered SOLELY on the basis of the following information.

Special Officers are responsible for monitoring and responding to radio messages, even if the officer is on meal break, performing clerical duties, or away from his post for other reasons. An officer shall answer radio messages directed to him during his tour.

23. Officer Lewis is chatting with friends in the cafeteria while on her scheduled meal break when she receives a radio message from Sergeant Baker. Sergeant Baker informs Officer Lewis that trouble has broken out at Location A and directs her to report to Location A immediately to assist the officers on the scene. Officer Lewis leaves the cafeteria immediately and reports to the scene.
Officer Lewis' action in response to Sergeant Baker's radio message is 23.____

   A. *correct,* chiefly because Officer Lewis is responsible for responding to all radio messages
   B. *incorrect,* chiefly because Officer Lewis is on meal break and therefore *off-duty*
   C. *correct,* chiefly because Officer Lewis was not doing anything important during her meal break
   D. *incorrect,* chiefly because the situation was not declared a *total emergency*

Question 24.

DIRECTIONS: Question 24 is to be answered SOLELY on the basis of the following information.

Special Officers must immediately report to their supervisor any incident or condition in the facility that may cause danger or inconvenience to the public.

24. Special Officer Scott is patrolling a small, crowded waiting room in his facility when two male clients start arguing with each other, shoving chairs around and frightening the other clients. Officer Scott intervenes in the argument, issues summonses for Disorderly Conduct to the individuals involved in the dispute, and escorts them off the premises. Officer Scott then records the incident in his memo book and resumes patrol.
In this situation, the FIRST action that Officer Scott should have taken when he observed the argument start between the two men is to 24.____

   A. call for help from Special Officers on nearby posts to restrain the men who were fighting
   B. report the incident to his supervisor immediately
   C. attempt to separate the men who were fighting in order to stop the fight
   D. evacuate the waiting room so that innocent bystanders would not be injured

Question 25.

DIRECTIONS: Question 25 is to be answered SOLELY on the basis of the following information.

An Officer on duty in a facility must remain on post until properly relieved. If not properly relieved as scheduled, he must notify his immediate supervisor by radio of this fact and follow the supervisor's instructions.

25. Officer Clough is working on an 8:00 A.M. to 4:00 P.M. tour. Officer Clough is to be relieved at 4:00 P.M. by Security Officer Crandall, who works the 4:00 P.M. to 12:00 Midnight shift. However, as of 4:15 P.M., Officer Crandall has not appeared to relieve Officer Clough, so Officer Clough leaves his post to find Officer Crandall. In this situation, Officer Clough's action is

    A. *correct,* chiefly because his tour was over and he wanted to go home
    B. *incorrect,* chiefly because he should have notified his supervisor of Officer Crandall's failure to relieve him
    C. *correct,* chiefly because Officer Clough is attempting to locate Officer Crandall so that the post will be covered
    D. *incorrect,* chiefly because Officer Clough should have left his post as soon as his tour ended rather than working any overtime

Questions 26-28.

DIRECTIONS: Questions 26 through 28 are to be answered SOLELY on the basis of the following information.

A summons is a written notice that a person is accused of violating a code or regulation. Special Officers have the authority to issue summonses to individuals for on-premises parking or traffic violations, or violations of the City Administrative Code. Summonses for violations of the Penal Law, such as for Disorderly Conduct, may also be issued.

The following is a list of types of summonses issued for violations and their descriptions:

Type of Summons	Description of Violation
Class A	Parking in fire lanes
Class A	Parking in space reserved for the handicapped
Class A	Vehicle blocking driveway
Class B	Disobeying stop sign
Class C	Disorderly Conduct
Class C	Harassment
Environmental Control Board	Smoking Violations
Environmental Control Board	Public Health Code

26. While on patrol, Special Officer Gladys Jones observes a parked car that is blocking a driveway.
She should issue a summons for a violation which is a

    A. Class A type   B. Class B type
    C. Class C type   D. Environmental Control Board

27. A man drives up to a facility, parks his car in a fire lane, and quickly runs inside the facility. An attempt to follow and locate the man is unsuccessful.
    Which one of the following is the type of summons that the Special Officer on duty should issue?

    A. Class A
    B. Class B
    C. Class C
    D. Environmental Control Board

28. While on patrol, Special Officer Mason observes a visitor smoking a cigarette in an area where smoking is prohibited. Officer Mason asks the visitor to stop smoking and shows him the *No Smoking* sign posted. The visitor refuses to comply.
    Officer Mason should issue which type of summons?

    A. Class A
    B. Class B
    C. Class C
    D. Environmental Control Board

Questions 29-31.

DIRECTIONS: Questions 29 through 31 are to be answered SOLELY on the basis of the following information and the Summons Form and Fact Pattern.

Special Officers must complete a summons form by filling in the appropriate information. A completed summons must include the name and address of the accused; license or other identification number; vehicle identification; the section number of the code, regulation, or law violated; a brief description of the violation; any scheduled fine; information about the time and place of occurrence; and the name, rank, and signature of the Special Officer issuing the summons.

The information listed on the Summons Form may or may not be correct.

SUMMONS FORM

LINE		
1	NOTICE OF VIOLATION No. 5 56784989	THE PEOPLE OF THE STATE OF NEW YORK VS. _____ OPERATOR PRESENT NO (YES) REFUSED ID
2	LAST NAME *Tucker*	FIRST NAME *James* MIDDLE INITIAL *T*
3	STREET ADDRESS *205 E. 53rd Street*	
4	CITY (AS SHOWN ON LICENSE) *Brooklyn, NY 11234*	
5	DRIVER LICENSE OR IDENTIFICATION NO. *J-7156907834*	STATE *NY* CLASS *5* DATE EXPIRES *1/12/13*
6	SEX *M*	DATE OF BIRTH *1/12/65*
7	LICENSE PLATE NO. *CVR-632* STATE *NY* DATE EXPIRES *8/12/12*	OPERATOR OWN VEHICLE? (YES) NO
8	BODY TYPE *Sedan* MAKE *Dodge*	COLOR *Green*
	THE PERSON DESCRIBED ABOVE IS CHARGED AS FOLLOWS:	
9	ISSUE TIME *9:30 A.M.* DATE OF OFFENSE *2/5/12* TIME FIRST OBSERVED *9:28 A.M.*	COUNTY *Kings*
10	PLACE OF OCCURRENCE *451 Clarkson Ave., Brooklyn, NY*	PRECINCT *71st*
11	IN VIOLATION OF SECTION *81-B* CODE *40* LAW *New York State Traffic Regulation*	
12	DESCRIPTION OF VIOLATION *Vehicle parked in front of a fire hydrant*	
13	SCHEDULED FINE $10 $15 $20 $25 $30 ($40) Other $___	
14	RANK/NAME OF ISSUING OFFICER *Special Officer Joseph Robbins*	SIGNATURE OF ISSUING OFFICER *Joseph Robbins*

12 (#1)

FACT PATTERN

On February 5, 2012, at 9:28 A.M., Special Officer Joseph Robbins is patrolling the grounds of the Brooklyn Hills Income Maintenance Center, located at 451 Clarkson Ave., Brooklyn, NY, when he observes an unoccupied parked vehicle blocking a fire hydrant near the facility's entrance. As Officer Robbins begins to write up a summons for the violation, James Tucker, the owner of the vehicle, emerges from the facility and comes over. While getting in his car, he asks why he is getting a summons. Officer Robbins explains to Mr. Tucker that he is in violation of traffic regulations pertaining to access to fire hydrants and asks him for identification. Mr. Tucker gives Officer Robbins his driver's license, showing the following information:

Name:	Tucker, James T.
Address:	205 E. 53rd Street, Brooklyn, NY 11234
Date of Birth:	January 12, 1965
Driver's License:	J-7156907894
Driver License Expiration Date:	January 12, 2013
Class:	5

29. The *place of occurrence* of the violation described in the Fact Pattern is on line _____ of the Summons Form.

    A. 2   B. 3   C. 8   D. 10

30. Which one of the following lines on the Summons Form shows information that does NOT agree with information given in the Fact Pattern?

    A. 1   B. 2   C. 4   D. 5

31. Which of the following is the date on which the violation occurred?

    A. 1/12/12   B. 2/5/12   C. 8/12/12   D. 1/12/13

32. Following are two sentences which may or may not be written in correct English:
    I. Two clients assaulted the officer.
    II. The van is illegally parked.
    Which one of the following statements is CORRECT?

    A. Only Sentence I is written in correct English.
    B. Only Sentence II is written in correct English.
    C. Sentences I and II are both written in correct English.
    D. Neither Sentence I nor Sentence II is written in correct English.

33. Following are two sentences which may or may not be written in correct English:
    I. Security Officer Rollo escorted the visitor to the patrolroom.
    II. Two entry were made in the facility logbook.
    Which one of the following statements is CORRECT?

    A. Only Sentence I is written in correct English.
    B. Only Sentence II is written in correct English.
    C. Sentences I and II are both written in correct English.
    D. Neither Sentence I nor Sentence II is written in correct English.

34. Following are two sentences which may or may not be written in correct English: 34.____
    I. Officer McElroy putted out a small fire in the wastepaper basket.
    II. Special Officer Janssen told the visitor where he could obtained a pass.
Which one of the following statements is CORRECT?

   A. Only Sentence I is written in correct English.
   B. Only Sentence II is written in correct English.
   C. Sentences I and II are both written in correct English.
   D. Neither Sentence I nor Sentence II are written in correct English.

35. Following are two sentences which may or may not be written in correct English: 35.____
    I. Security Officer Warren observed a broken window while he was on his post in Hallway C.
    II. The worker reported that two typewriters had been stoled from the office.
Which one of the following statements is CORRECT?

   A. Only Sentence I is written in correct English.
   B. Only Sentence II is written in correct English.
   C. Sentences I and II are both written in correct English.
   D. Neither Sentence I nor Sentence II is written in correct English.

KEY (CORRECT ANSWERS)

1.	C	16.	C
2.	A	17.	B
3.	D	18.	A
4.	B	19.	C
5.	C	20.	A
6.	B	21.	C
7.	D	22.	D
8.	A	23.	A
9.	B	24.	B
10.	B	25.	B
11.	C	26.	A
12.	C	27.	A
13.	C	28.	D
14.	B	29.	D
15.	A	30.	D

31.	B
32.	C
33.	A
34.	D
35.	A

TEST 2

DIRECTIONS: Each question or incomplete statement is followed by several suggested answers or completions. Select the one that BEST answers the question or completes the statement. *PRINT THE LETTER OF THE CORRECT ANSWER IN THE SPACE AT THE RIGHT.*

Questions 1-5.

DIRECTIONS: Questions 1 through 5 are to be answered SOLELY on the basis of the following information.

Special Officers have the power to arrest members of the public who commit crimes in violation of the Penal Law. Assume that certain classes of crimes covered by various sections of the Penal Law are described below. Special Officers must be able to apply this information when making an arrest in order to accurately determine the type of crime that has been committed.

Crime	Class of Crime	Description of Crime	Section
Petit Larceny	A Misdemeanor	Stealing property worth up to $250	155.25
Grand Larceny 3rd Degree	E Felony	Stealing property worth more than $250	155.30
Grand Larceny 2nd Degree	D Felony	Stealing property worth more than $1,500	155.35
Grand Larceny 1st Degree	C Felony	Stealing property worth any amount of money while making a person fear injury or damage to property	155.40
Assault 3rd Degree	A Misdemeanor	Injuring a person	120.00
Assault 2nd Degree	D Felony	1. Seriously injuring a person; or 2. Injuring an officer of the law	120.05
Assault 1st Degree	C Felony	Seriously injuring a person using a deadly or dangerous weapon	120.10
Disorderly Conduct	Violation	1. Engages in fighting or threatening behavior; or 2. Makes unreasonable noise	240.20
Robbery 3rd Degree	D Felony	Stealing property by force	160.05
Robbery 2nd Degree	C Felony	1. Stealing property by force with the help of another person; or 2. Stealing property by force and injuring any person	160.10
Robbery 1st Degree	B Felony	Stealing property by force and seriously injuring the owner of property	160.15

1. Which one of the following crimes is considered to be Class A Misdemeanor? 1.____

    A. Grand Larceny - 3rd Degree
    B. Grand Larceny - 2nd Degree
    C. Assault - 3rd Degree
    D. Assault - 2nd Degree

2. Which one of the following crimes is considered to be Class B Felony? 2.____

    A. Robbery - 2nd Degree
    B. Robbery - 1st Degree
    C. Grand Larceny - 3rd Degree
    D. Grand Larceny - 2nd Degree

3. A worker at a facility reports that a typewriter worth $400 has been stolen from her office. Which one of the following is the type of crime that has been committed? 3.____

    A. Grand Larceny - 3rd Degree
    B. Grand Larceny - 2nd Degree
    C. Grand Larceny - 1st Degree
    D. Petit Larceny

4. A visitor at a facility begins yelling very loudly at a receptionist and shakes his fist at her. The visitor refuses to stop yelling when an officer tries to calm him down, and he shakes his fist at the officer. Which one of the following is the type of crime that occurred? 4.____

    A. Assault - 3rd Degree   B. Assault - 2nd Degree
    C. Assault - 1st Degree   D. Disorderly Conduct

5. An officer has apprehended and arrested a visitor who was attempting to leave the facility with a radio he had stolen from an office. The radio is worth $100. 5.____
Under which one of the following sections of the Penal Law should the visitor be charged? Section

    A. 155.25   B. 155.30   C. 155.35   D. 155.40

Questions 6-12.

DIRECTIONS: Questions 6 through 12 are to be answered SOLELY on the basis of the Arrest Report Form and Incident Report shown on the following page. These reports were submitted by Special Officer John Clark, Shield #512, to his supervisor, Sergeant Joseph Lewis, Shield #818, of the North Bay Health Clinic

Special Officers are required to complete both an Arrest Report Form and an Incident Report whenever an unusual incident or an arrest occurs. The Arrest Report Form provides detailed information regarding the victim and the person arrested, along with a brief description of the incident.

The Incident Report provides a detailed description of the incident. Both reports include the following information: WHO was involved in the incident, including witnesses; WHAT happened and HOW it happened; WHERE and WHEN the incident occurred; and WHY the incident occurred.

ARREST REPORT FORM

ARREST INFORMATION (1)	TIME OF OCCURRENCE 11:15 A.M.	DATE OF OCCURRENCE February 1, 2012	DAY OF WEEK Monday	
INFORMATION ABOUT VICTIM (2)	VICTIM'S NAME Darlene Kirk		ADDRESS 7855 Cruger St., Bronx, NY 10488	
(3)	SEX F	DATE OF BIRTH 9/3/75	RACE White	HOME TELEPHONE # 212-733-3462	SOCIAL SECURITY # 245-63-0772
INFORMATION ABOUT PERSON ARRESTED (4)	NAME OF PERSON ARRESTED Elsie Gardner		ADDRESS 2447 Southern Pkway, Bronx, NY 10467	
(5)	SEX F	DATE OF BIRTH 7/9/80	RACE White	HOME TELEPHONE # 212-513-7029	SOCIAL SECURITY # 244-08-0569
(6)	HEIGHT 5'5"	WEIGHT 135 lbs.	HAIR COLOR Brown	CLOTHING Black coat/red pants	
DESCRIPTION OF CRIME (7)	SECTION OF PENAL LAW 120.00		TYPE OF CRIME Assault - 3rd Degree		
(8)	TIME OF ARREST 11:35 A.M.	DATE OF ARREST 2/1/12	LOCATION OF ARREST 635 Bay Avenue Bronx, NY		
(9)	DESCRIPTION OF INCIDENT The defendant, Elsie Gardner, struck the victim after the victim requested that Ms. Gardner stop smoking in a "NO SMOKING" area. Two witnesses verified the victim's account of the incident.				
INFORMATION ABOUT ARRESTING OFFICER (10)	REPORTING OFFICER'S SIGNATURE John Clark		NAME PRINTED John Clark		
(11)	RANK Special Officer		SHIELD NUMBER 512		

INCIDENT REPORT

(1) At 11:15 A.M. on February 1, 2012, I was directed by Sergeant Mark Lewis via two-way radio to report to the Nutrition Clinic on the 4th Floor to investigate a disturbance. (2) Special Officer Anna Colon, Shield #433, was directed to assist me. (3) At 11:16 A.M., Officer Colon and I arrived at the Health Clinic and observed a patient, Elsie Gardner, repeatedly strike Health Clinic receptionist Darlene Kirk about the head and neck. (4) Officer Colon restrained Ms. Gardner while I placed handcuffs on her wrists. (5) Ms. Kirk complained that her neck felt sore. (6) After being examined by Dr. Stone, Ms. Kirk told us that Ms. Gardner entered the Health Clinic at approximately 11:10 A.M. and lit a cigarette in the waiting area. (7) At 11:20 A.M., Dr. Paul Stone examined Ms. Kirk. (8) Ms. Kirk explained to Ms. Gardner that smoking was not allowed in the Health Clinic and showed her the NO SMOKING signs posted on the walls. (9) Ms. Gardner ignored Ms. Kirk, and then grew very abusive and attacked her when Ms. Kirk insisted that she stop smoking. (10) Two witnesses, patients Edna Manning of 8937 4th Ave., Bronx, NY, and John Schultz of 357 149th Street, Bronx, NY, gave the same account of the incident as Ms. Kirk. (11) At 11:30 A.M., I read the prisoner her rights and placed her under arrest for violation of Penal Law Section 120.00 -Assault 3rd Degree. (12) At 11:35 A.M., I notified the 86th Precinct of Ms. Gardner's arrest and arranged for the transportation of the prisoner to the precinct. (13) At 11:40 A.M., Officer Colon escorted Ms. Gardner from the Nutrition Clinic to the patrolroom. (14) At 11:55 A.M., Police Officers Cranford, Shield #658, and Wargo, Shield #313, arrived at the facility to transport the prisoner to the precinct. (15) Officer Gray, Shield #936, assumed my post while I reported to the patrolroom to complete the necessary forms concerning the arrest.

6. At what time did Sergeant Lewis inform Officer John Clark of the disturbance in the Nutrition Clinic?
_____ A.M.

   A. 11:00   B. 11:15   C. 11:16   D. 11:20

7. According to the Arrest Report and the Incident Report, how many witnesses gave the same account of the incident as Ms. Kirk?

   A. 1   B. 2   C. 3   D. 4

8. What information on the Arrest Report is NOT included in the Incident Report?

   A. Date of Occurrence
   B. Victim's address
   C. Section of the Penal Law violated
   D. Assault 3rd Degree

9. Which sentence in the Incident Report is out of order in terms of the sequence of events?

   A. 3   B. 6   C. 11   D. 12

10. According to the Incident Report, at 11:40 A.M. Ms. Gardner was

    A. escorted to the patrolroom
    B. transported to the 86th Precinct
    C. examined by Dr. Paul Stone
    D. giving an account of the incident to Special Officers Clark and Colon

11. According to the Incident Report, which one of the following officers relieved Officer Clark?
    Officer

    A. Colon   B. Cranford   C. Wargo   D. Gray

12. Which section of the Arrest Report contains information that does NOT agree with Sentence 11 of the Incident Report?
    Section

    A. 1   B. 7   C. 8   D. 9

Question 13.

DIRECTIONS: Question 13 is to be answered SOLELY on the basis of the following information.

A Security Officer must investigate any complaint or incident which occurs in the facility, whether he considers it is major or minor. The Officer must also interview the person(s) involved in the incident in order to complete the necessary forms and reports.

13. Ms. Peters, a clerical worker at the facility, complains to Officer Tynan that a pen set, which had been given to her as a gift, was missing from her desk. She tells Officer Tynan that she knows the pen set was on her desk the previous day because she was using it for her work. Officer Tynan informs Ms. Peters that there is nothing he can do since the pen set was personal property and not facility property.
In this situation, Officer Tynan's response to Ms. Peters is

13.____

   A. *correct,* chiefly because the pen set should not have been left out on a desk where it could be stolen
   B. *incorrect,* chiefly because a complaint of a loss of theft should be investigated and recorded
   C. *correct,* chiefly because Special Officers are only required to investigate a loss or theft of facility property
   D. *incorrect,* chiefly because Ms. Peters' work required use of the pen set

Question 14.

DIRECTIONS: Question 14 is to be answered SOLELY on the basis of the following information.

Assume that Security Officers are responsible for recording in a personal memobook all of their routine and non-routine activities and occurrences for each tour of duty. Before starting a tour of duty, a Security Officer must enter in his personal memobook the date, tour, and assigned post. An entry shall be made to record each absence from duty, such as a regular day off, sick leave, annual leave, or holiday. During each tour, a Security Officer shall enter a full and accurate record of duties performed, changes in post assignment, absences from post, and the reason for each absence, and all other patrol business.

14. Security Officer Ella Lewis is assigned to Gotham Center Facility, where she works Monday through Friday on a 9:00 A.M. to 5:00 P.M. tour. Officer Lewis' regular days off are Saturday and Sunday. Officer Lewis worked on Wednesday, November 25, 2012. She was absent on Thursday, November 26, 2012, for Thanksgiving Holiday, and on Friday, November 27, 2012, for annual leave.
According to the information given above, which of the following entries is the FIRST entry that Officer Lewis should record in her memobook when she returns to work on November 30, 2012?

14.____

   A. Saturday, 11/28/12 and Sunday, 11/29/12 - Regular days off
   B. Friday, 11/27/12 - Sick Leave
   C. Monday, 11/30/12 - On duty
   D. Thursday, 11/26/12 - Thanksgiving Holiday

Questions 15-16.

DIRECTIONS: Questions 15 and 16 are to be answered SOLELY on the basis of the following entries recorded by Security Officer Angela Russo in her memobook.

Date: January 8, 2012
Tour: 8:00 A.M. to 4:00 P.M.
Weather: Sunny and clear

7:30	Reported to *B* Command for Roll Call. Assigned to Post #2, *C* Building Emergency Room Corridor by Sergeant Robert Floyd. Break: 9:30 A.M. Meal: 1:30 P.M. Radio: #701
7:40	Arrived at Post #2 and relieved Special Officer Johnson, Shield #593.
7:45	On patrol - Post #2.
8:00	Post #2 - All secure at this time; conditions normal.
8:30	Fire Alarm Box 5-3-1 rings on 3rd Floor South in *C* Building. Upon arrival, Office Worker Molly Lewis reported that a waste-paper basket was on fire. Used fire extinguisher to put out fire.
8:50	Condition corrected; Incident Report prepared and submitted to Sergeant Floyd in *B* Command.
8:55	Resumed patrol of Post #2.
9:30	Relieved for break by Officer Tucker.
9:50	Resumed patrol of Post #2.
10:10	Disorderly person reported by Clinic Director Lila Jones on Ward C-32; Officer Bailey and myself responded. Clinic Director Jones informed officers that visitor Bradley Manna, male white, 19 years of age, 2 Park Place, Brooklyn, NY, is drunk and has been shouting insults to Clinic staff.
10:30	Condition corrected; Visitor Bradley Manna escorted off premises. *B* Command notified of incident.
10:40	Resumed patrol of Post #2.
11:40	Post #2 - All secure at this time.
12:40	Post #2 - All secure at this time.

15. The name of the Clinic Director who reported a disorderly person is   15._____

    A. Molly Lewis   B. Bradley Manna
    C. Lila Jones   D. Robert Floyd

16. Which of the following sets of officers responded to the report of a disorderly person on   16._____
Ward C-32?
Officers

    A. Johnson and Bailey   B. Russo and Tucker
    C. Johnson and Tucker   D. Russo and Bailey

17. Security Officer Mace is completing an entry in her memo-book. The entry has the following five sentences:
    1. I observed the defendant removing a radio from a facility vehicle.
    2. I placed the defendant under arrest and escorted him to the patrolroom.
    3. I was patrolling the facility parking lot.
    4. I asked the defendant to show identification.
    5. I determined that the defendant was not authorized to remove the radio.

    The MOST logical order for these sentences to be entered in Officer Mace's memo-book is

    A. 1, 3, 2, 4, 5
    B. 2, 5, 4, 1, 3
    C. 3, 1, 4, 5, 2
    D. 4, 5, 2, 1, 3

18. Security Officer Riley is completing an entry in his memo-book. The entry has the following five sentences:
    1. Anna Jones admitted that she stole Mary Green's wallet.
    2. I approached the women and asked them who they were and why they were arguing.
    3. I arrested Anna Jones for stealing Mary Green's wallet.
    4. They identified themselves and Mary Green accused Anna Jones of stealing her wallet.
    5. I was in the lobby area when I observed two women arguing about a wallet.

    The MOST logical order for these sentences to be entered in Officer Riley's memobook is

    A. 2, 4, 1, 3, 5
    B. 3, 1, 4, 5, 2
    C. 4, 1, 5, 2, 3
    D. 5, 2, 4, 1, 3

19. Assume that Security Officer John Ryan is completing an entry in his memobook. The entry has the following five sentences:
    1. I then cleared the immediate area of visitors and staff.
    2. I noticed smoke coming from a broom closet outside Room A71.
    3. Sergeant Mueller arrived with other officers to assist in clearing the area.
    4. Upon investigation, I determined the smoke was due to burning material in the broom closet.
    5. I pulled the corridor fire alarm and notified Sergeant Mueller of the fire.

    The MOST logical order for these sentences to be entered in Officer Ryan's memo-book is

    A. 2, 3, 4, 5, 1
    B. 2, 4, 5, 1, 3
    C. 4, 1, 2, 3, 5
    D. 5, 3, 2, 1, 4

20. Security Officer Hernandez is completing an entry in his memobook. The entry has the following five sentences:
    1. I asked him to leave the premises immediately.
    2. A visitor complained that there was a strange man loitering in Clinic B hallway.
    3. I went to investigate and saw a man dressed in rags sitting on the floor of the hallway.
    4. As he walked out, he started yelling that he had no place to go.
    5. I asked to see identification, but he said that he did not have any.

    The MOST logical order for these sentences to be entered in Officer Hernandez's memobook is

A. 2, 3, 5, 1, 4 B. 3, 1, 2, 4, 5
C. 4, 1, 5, 2, 3 D. 3, 1, 5, 2, 4

21. Officer Hogan is completing an entry in his memobook. The entry has the following five sentences:
    1. When the fighting had stopped, I transmitted a message requesting medical assistance for Mr. Perkins.
    2. Special Officer Manning assisted me in stopping the fight.
    3. When I arrived at the scene, I saw a client, Adam Finley strike a facility employee, Peter Perkins.
    4. As I attempted to break up the fight, Special Officer Manning came on the scene.
    5. I received a radio message from Sergeant Valez to investigate a possible fight in progress in the waiting room.

    The MOST logical order for these sentences to be entered in Officer Hogan's memo-book is

    A. 2, 1, 4, 5, 3   B. 3, 5, 2, 4, 1
    C. 4, 5, 3, 1, 2   D. 5, 3, 4, 2, 1

Questions 22-23.

DIRECTIONS: Questions 22 and 23 are to be answered SOLELY on the basis of the following information.

Assume that Security Officers may be assigned to the facility patrolroom and must follow the guidelines below in documenting all routine and non-routine activities and occurrences in the facility logbook.

At the beginning of each tour of duty, the Security Officer responsible for entering information in the logbook must transfer from the Roll Call Sheet to the logbook a list of all security staff personnel assigned to that tour. This list is to be entered in order of the rank of the security staff member. All other entries in the facility logbook shall be recorded in chronological order, in blue or black ink, and be neat and legible.

22. When recording the list of security staff personnel assigned to a tour, that entry shall be made in

    A. chronological order
    B. order of rank of security staff
    C. alphabetical order
    D. order of arrival at facility

23. A Security Officer has transmitted notification to the patrolroom that he has just issued a summons. The Security Officer responsible for documenting occurrences in the patrolroom logbook should record the information

    A. in red ink, immediately following the previous entry
    B. on a new page under the heading *Summonses Reported*
    C. in blue or black ink immediately following the previous entry
    D. on the last page of the logbook where it can be easily found

Question 24.

DIRECTIONS: Question 24 is to be answered SOLELY on the basis of the following information.

Assume that whenever a Security Officer is to begin a leave of absence, long-term sick leave, or other type of leave having an anticipated length of ten days or more, the officer shall surrender his or her security shield to his supervisor, who shall immediately forward it to Security Headquarters.

24. Two male clients were fighting in the waiting room of North End Hospital. Officer Gary Klott attempted to separate them and became involved in the altercation. Officer Klott sustained an injury to the right eye and was examined by a physician. The physician directed Officer Klott to stay home for a recovery period of 12 days. In this situation, Officer Klott should

    A. surrender his shield to his supervisor
    B. safeguard his shield in a safe place at home while he is recovering
    C. surrender his shield to the physician
    D. safeguard his shield with his uniform in his locker at the facility while he is recovering

Question 25.

DIRECTIONS: Question 25 is to be answered SOLELY on the basis of the following information.

Assume that Security Officers are required to follow certain procedures when on post at a restricted area of a facility. They must inspect the identification of employees and passes of visitors, as well as all bags and packages carried by individuals who wish to enter the restricted area.

25. Security Officer Stevens is assigned to a post at the Intensive Care Unit of Park View Hospital, a restricted area. Officer Stevens is responsible for inspecting identification and passes, as well as all bags and packages carried by individuals who want to enter the Unit. He sees Mr. Craig approach. He knows Mr. Craig's wife is a patient in the Unit. Officer Stevens has seen Mr. Craig visit his wife every day for the past four days. Mr. Craig brings a small duffel bag filled with magazines each time he comes. Today, Officer Stevens checks Mr. Craig's visitor's pass but lets Mr. Craig enter the Unit without checking his duffel bag. In this situation, Officer Stevens' action is

    A. *correct*, chiefly because he has checked to see that Mr. Craig has a visitor's pass
    B. *incorrect*, chiefly because all packages and bags must be inspected before anyone is allowed to enter a restricted area
    C. *correct,* chiefly because he is familiar with Mr. Craig and knows that he only carries magazines in his duffel bag
    D. *incorrect*, chiefly because Mr. Craig should not be allowed to carry a bag or package into a restricted area of the facility

Question 26.

DIRECTIONS: Question 26 is to be answered SOLELY on the basis of the following information.

Assume that Special Officers must safeguard evidence in cases involving firearms. Special Officers must mark recovered bullets for identification purposes. The Officer who recovers the bullet must mark his or her initials and the date of recovery of the bullet on the base or on the nose of the bullet.

26. On January 18, 2012, at 11:30 P.M., an unidentified person fired a shot at an unoccupied security patrol car in the facility parking lot. Officer Debra Johnson was assigned to investigate the matter. A fired bullet was recovered inside the patrol car by Officer Johnson at 1:00 A.M. on January 19, 2012.
Officer Johnson should mark *D.J. 1/19/12* on

    A. the base or the nose of the recovered bullet
    B. the side of the recovered bullet
    C. an envelope and place the recovered bullet inside
    D. the side of the patrol car from which the bullet was recovered

Question 27.

DIRECTIONS: Question 27 is to be answered SOLELY on the basis of the following information.

Patrolroom Observers are officers who are assigned to observe events when individuals, other than security staff, are present in the patrolroom. According to facility guidelines, a Patrolroom Observer must be called to the patrolroom to serve as a witness whenever any individual is brought to the patrolroom for any reason by a Special Officer.

27. Janet Childs, a client at Gotham Health Facility, was robbed in the facility's parking lot. Ms. Childs was not harmed as a result of the incident, but she was upset. Special Officer Grey escorted her to the patrol-room, where she remained until she felt better. While she was waiting in the patrolroom, Officer Grey did not call a Patrolman Observer to the patrolroom during the time that Ms. Childs was there.
In this situation, Officer Grey

    A. should not have taken Ms. Childs to the patrolroom without special authorization from his supervisor
    B. was not required to call a Patrolroom Observer to the patrolroom since Ms. Childs had not been placed under arrest
    C. should have called a Patrolroom Observer to be present while Ms. Childs was in the patrolroom
    D. should have escorted Ms. Childs to the patrolroom and left her in the care of the Special Officer assigned to the patrolroom

Question 28.

DIRECTIONS: Question 28 is to be answered SOLELY on the basis of the following information.

Special Officers escort individuals categorized as Emotionally Disturbed Persons to the hospital for observation or treatment when directed to do so. These individuals are transported to the hospital by Emergency Medical Service (EMS) ambulance. There must be one Special Officer present in the ambulance for each Emotionally Disturbed Person transferred to the hospital, along with an EMS Technician and the ambulance driver.

28. Special Officers Patrick Lawson and Grace Martin have been assigned to escort two individuals categorized as Emotionally Disturbed Persons from that facility to a nearby hospital. The EMS ambulance, with an EMS Technician and ambulance driver, has arrived at the facility to transport the individuals. Officer Lawson then suggests to Officer Martin that it is not necessary for him to go to the hospital since the EMS Technician will be with Officer Martin in the ambulance.
In this situation, Officer Lawson's suggestion is

    A. *correct,* since an EMS Technician will be present in the ambulance to accompany Officer Martin and the Emotionally Disturbed Persons to the hospital
    B. *incorrect,* since one Special Officer must be present in the ambulance for each Emotionally Disturbed Person transported to the hospital
    C. *correct,* since the Emotionally Disturbed Persons are unlikely to cause any disturbance inside the ambulance
    D. *incorrect,* since two EMS Technicians must be present in the ambulance when only one Special Officer is escorting two Emotionally Disturbed Persons to the hospital

28.____

Questions 29-32.

DIRECTIONS: Questions 29 through 32 are to be answered on the basis of the following information.

Assume that information concerning new or updated policies and procedures are sometimes provided to facility security staff in the form of a memorandum from Security Headquarters.

Question 29.

DIRECTIONS: Question 29 is to be answered SOLELY on the basis of the following memorandum.

TO: All Security Officers
FROM: Security Headquarters
SUBJECT: Smoking Regulations

At times, Security Officers have been observed smoking while on duty at their assigned posts. This is strictly prohibited. If Officers feel that they must smoke, they may smoke during breaks or lunch period in designated areas. Officers may not smoke while on official duty. If any Officer is observed smoking while on post or while performing official duties, appropriate disciplinary action will be taken.

29. According to the above memorandum, Security Officers may

   A. smoke while on duty, as long as they are out of view of the public
   B. not smoke while on duty except when assigned to a post in a designated smoking area
   C. smoke on breaks or during lunch period in designated areas
   D. not smoke at any time when dressed in official uniform

Question 30.

DIRECTIONS: Question 30 is to be answered SOLELY on the basis of the following memorandum.

TO: All Special Officers
FROM: Security Headquarters
SUBJECT: Safeguarding Shields and Identification Cards

Special Officers must ensure that their shields and identification cards are secure at all times. Should an officer become aware of the loss or theft of his shield or identification card, he shall immediately report such loss or theft to Security Headquarters.

30. According to the above memorandum, a Special Officer must

   A. report the loss or theft of his identification card to the nearest police precinct
   B. secure his shield in his locker at all times
   C. report the loss or theft of his shield or identification card to Security Headquarters immediately
   D. secure his identification card at Security Headquarters each night before leaving the facility

Question 31.

DIRECTIONS: Question 31 is to be answered SOLELY on the basis of the following memorandum.

TO: All Security Officers
FROM: Security Headquarters
SUBJECT: Fire in the Facility

Special Officers must report immediately to assist at the scene of a fire when directed to do so by a supervisor. Officers shall remain at the scene and ensure that only authorized personnel are in an area restricted by a fire emergency. Visitors and clients shall be directed to the nearest safe stairwell and out of the facility. Visitors and clients are not to use elevators to evacuate the area.

31. According to the above memorandum, a Security Officer should

   A. direct visitors and clients to the nearest elevator in case of fire
   B. report unauthorized personnel at a fire scene to the Fire Department
   C. escort visitors and clients down the nearest stairwell and out of the facility
   D. ensure that only authorized personnel are in an area restricted by a fire emergency

Question 32.

DIRECTIONS: Question 32 is to be answered SOLELY on the basis of the following memorandum.

TO: All Security Officers
FROM: Security Headquarters
SUBJECT: Reporting Unsafe Conditions

Security Officers shall report to their supervisors and appropriate facility staff any condition that could affect the safety or security of the facility. Conditions such as broken windows, unlocked doors and water leaks should be reported.

32. According to the above memorandum, a Security Officer shall   32.____

   A. make recommendations to his superiors concerning other facility staff members
   B. correct all unsafe conditions such as broken windows
   C. report a condition such as a water leak to his supervisor and appropriate facility staff
   D. make recommendations to facility staff concerning doors to be left unlocked

33. Following are two sentences that may or may not be written in correct English: 33.____
   I. Special Officer Cleveland was attempting to calm an emotionally disturbed visitor.
   II. The visitor did not stops crying and calling for his wife.
   Which one of the following statements is CORRECT?

   A. Only Sentence I is written in correct English.
   B. Only Sentence II is written in correct English.
   C. Sentences I and II are both written in correct English.
   D. Neither Sentence I nor Sentence II is written in correct English.

34. Following are two sentences that may or may not be written in correct English: 34.____
   I. While on patrol, I observes a vagrant loitering near the drug dispensary.
   II. I escorted the vagrant out of the building and off the premises.
   Which one of the following statements is CORRECT?

   A. Only Sentence I is written in correct English.
   B. Only Sentence II is written in correct English.
   C. Sentences I and II are both written in correct English.
   D. Neither Sentence I nor Sentence II is written in correct English.

35. Following are two sentences that may or may not be written in correct English: 35.____
   I. At 4:00 P.M., Sergeant Raymond told me to evacuate the waiting area immediately due to a bomb threat.
   II. Some of the clients did not want to leave the building.
   Which one of the following statements is CORRECT?

   A. Only Sentence I is written in correct English.
   B. Only Sentence II is written in correct English.
   C. Sentences I and II are both written in correct English.
   D. Neither Sentence I nor Sentence II is written in correct English.

KEY (CORRECT ANSWERS)

1.	C	16.	D
2.	B	17.	C
3.	A	18.	D
4.	D	19.	B
5.	A	20.	A
6.	B	21.	D
7.	B	22.	B
8.	B	23.	C
9.	B	24.	A
10.	A	25.	B
11.	D	26.	A
12.	C	27.	C
13.	B	28.	B
14.	D	29.	C
15.	C	30.	C

31.	D
32.	C
33.	A
34.	B
35.	C

EXAMINATION SECTION
TEST 1

DIRECTIONS: Questions 1 through 5 are to be answered on the basis of the information, instructions, and sample question given below. Each question contains a GENERAL RULE, EXCEPTIONS, a PROBLEM, and the ACTION actually taken.

The GENERAL RULE explains what the special officer (security officer) should or should not do.

The EXCEPTIONS describe circumstances under which a special officer (security officer) should take action contrary to the GENERAL RULE.

However, an unusual emergency may justify taking an action that is not covered either by the GENERAL RULE or by the stated EXCEPTIONS.

The PROBLEM describes a situation requiring some action by the special officer (security officer).

ACTION describes what a special officer (security officer) actually did in that particular case.

Read carefully the GENERAL RULE and EXCEPTIONS, the PROBLEM, and the ACTION, and the mark A, B, C, or D in the space at the right in accordance with the following instructions:

I. If an action is clearly justified under the general rule, mark your answer A.
II. If an action is not justified under the general rule, but is justified under a stated exception, mark your answer B.
III. If an action is not justified either by the general rule or by a stated exception, but does seem strongly justified by an unusual emergency situation, mark your answer C.
IV. If an action does not seem justified for any of these reasons, mark your answer D.

SAMPLE QUESTION:

GENERAL RULE: A special officer (security officer) is not empowered to stop a person and search him for hidden weapons.
EXCEPTION: He may stop a person and search him if he has good reason to believe that he may be carrying a hidden weapon. Good reasons to believe he may be carrying a hidden weapon include (a) notification through official channels that a person may be armed, (b) a statement directly to the special officer (security officer) by the person himself that he is armed, and (c) the special officer's (security officer's) own direct observation.

PROBLEM: A special officer (security officer) on duty at a hospital clinic is notified by a woman patient at the clinic that a man sitting near her is making muttered threats that he has a gun and is going to shoot his doctor if the doctor gives him any trouble. Although the woman is upset, she seems to be telling the truth, and two other waiting patients con-

firm this. However, the special officer (security officer) approaches the man and sees no sign of a hidden weapon. The man tells the officer that he has no weapon.
ACTION: The special officer (security officer) takes the man aside into an empty office and proceeds to frisk him for a concealed weapon.

ANSWER: The answer cannot be A, because the general rule is that a special officer (security officer) is not empowered to search a person for hidden weapons. The answer cannot be B, because the notification did not come through official channels, the man did not tell the special officer (security officer) that he had a weapon, and the special officer (security officer) did not observe any weapon. However, since three people have confirmed that the man has said he has a weapon and is threatening to use it, this is pretty clearly an emergency situation that calls for action. Therefore, the answer is C.

1. GENERAL RULE: A special officer (security officer) on duty at a certain entrance is not to leave his post unguarded at any time.
 EXCEPTION: He may leave the post for a brief period if he first summons a replacement. He may also leave if it is necessary for him to take prompt emergency action to prevent injury to persons or property.
 PROBLEM: The special officer (security officer) sees a man running down a hall with a piece of iron pipe in his hand, chasing another man who is shouting for help. By going in immediate pursuit, there is a good chance that the special officer (security officer) can stop the man with the pipe.
 ACTION: The special officer (security officer) leaves his post unguarded and pursues the man.

 The CORRECT answer is:

 A. I   B. II   C. III   D. IV

2. GENERAL RULE: Special officers (security officers) assigned to a college campus are instructed not to arrest students for minor violations such as disorderly conduct; instead, the violation should be stopped and the incident should be reported to the college authorities, who will take disciplinary action.
 EXCEPTION: A special officer (security officer) may arrest a student or take other appropriate action if failure to do so is likely to result in personal injury or property damage, or disruption of school activities, or if the incident involves serious criminal behavior.
 PROBLEM: A special officer (security officer) is on duty in a college building where evening classes are being held. He is told that two students are causing a disturbance in a classroom. He arrives and finds that a fist fight is in progress and the classroom is in an uproar. The special officer (security officer) separates the two students who are fighting and takes them out of the room. Both of them seem to be intoxicated. They both have valid student ID cards.
 ACTION: The special officer (security officer) takes down their names and addresses for his report, then tells them to leave the building with a warning not to return this evening.

 The CORRECT answer is:

 A. I   B. II   C. III   D. IV

3. GENERAL RULE: A special officer (security officer) is not permitted to carry a gun while on duty.
EXCEPTION: A special officer (security officer) who disarms a person must keep the weapon in his possession for the brief period before he can turn it over to the proper authorities. A special officer (security officer) who is NOT on duty may, like any other citizen, own and carry a gun if he has a proper permit from the Police Department.
PROBLEM: A special officer (security officer) is assigned to a post where there have been a series of violent incidents in the past few days. He feels that these incidents could have been controlled much more easily if the people involved had seen that the special officer (security officer) had a gun. He has a gun at home, for which he has a valid permit.
ACTION: The special officer (security officer) brings his gun when he goes on duty. He does not plan to use it, but just show people that he has it so that they will not start any trouble.

The CORRECT answer is:

A. I B. II C. III D. IV

4. GENERAL RULE: No one except a licensed physician or someone acting directly under a physician's orders may legally administer medicine to another person.
EXCEPTION: In a first aid situation, the special officer (security officer) is allowed to help a person suffering frori a heart condition or other disease to take medicine which the person has in his possession, provided that the person is conscious and requests this assistance.
PROBLEM: A special officer (security officer) on duty at a public building is told that a man has collapsed in the elevator. When the special officer (security officer) arrives at the scene, the man is barely conscious. He cannot speak, but he points to his pocket. The special officer (security officer) finds a pill bottle that says *one capsule in ease of need*. The man nods.
ACTION: The special officer (security officer) puts one capsule in the man's hand and guides the man's hand to his mouth.

The CORRECT answer is:

A. I B. II C. III D. IV

5. GENERAL RULE: In case of a fire drill or fire alarm, special officers (security officers) on patrol in a building are to remain in their assigned areas to assist in the evacuation of persons from the building and to make sure that no one takes advantage of the situation by stealing property that is left unguarded.
EXCEPTION: Should there be an actual fire, special officers (security officers) will follow whatever instructions are given by the firefighters or police officers who arrive on the scene to take charge.
PROBLEM: A special officer (security officer) is on duty patroling the fifth floor of a building when a fire alarm sounds. The fire is in a supply closet at one end of the fifth floor. All personnel have been evacuated from the floor. Neither police nor firemen have yet shown up.
ACTION: The special officer (security officer) stays on the fifth floor at a safe distance from the supply closet.

The CORRECT answer is:

A. I B. II C. III D. IV

KEY (CORRECT ANSWERS)

1. B
2. A
3. D
4. B
5. A

EXAMINATION SECTION
TEST 1

DIRECTIONS: Each question or incomplete statement is followed by several suggested answers or completions. Select the one that BEST answers the question or completes the statement. *PRINT THE LETTER OF THE CORRECT ANSWER IN THE SPACE AT THE RIGHT.*

1. When training your subordinates in a new method of crowd control, which one of the following techniques SHOULD be used?

    A. Teach them the whole job at one time, whether it contains a great many steps or only a few
    B. Issue orders without giving reasons because this will result in more questions and delays
    C. Explain and demonstrate, one step at a time
    D. Use technical language in order to make instructions precise

2. It is sometimes necessary to provide additional training for staff members who are poor in their performance of specific tasks.
   Of the following, the MOST effective way of improving staff performance is to

    A. use visual aids along with reading material to train staff on the general subject involved
    B. train subordinates to perform only those tasks which they normally perform
    C. plan and carry out programs to meet the subordinates' real work needs
    D. provide training only for staff members performing critical tasks

3. Assume that as a superior officer you confront one of your subordinate officers with the fact that he is not performing his job effectively. The officer tries to avoid the blame and shifts the criticism to other officers including yourself.
   Which one of the following is NOT a good way of handling this situation?

    A. Speaking and acting in an impartial and fair-minded manner
    B. Trying to determine why the officer finds it difficult to accept justifiable criticism
    C. Calling in the other officers whom this subordinate has criticized and having them discuss the matter with him
    D. Listening to the officer, at least at the outset, rather than interrupting his statement

4. For a superior officer to discuss a subordinate's performance evaluation with him is GENERALLY

    A. *inadvisable;* such a discussion will discourage a good worker
    B. *advisable;* the subordinate must know about the quality of his performance for improvement to occur
    C. *inadvisable;* a good performance evaluation will result in the subordinate's asking for more responsibility
    D. *advisable;* such discussions generally lead to a change in the subordinate's evaluation

1.____

2.____

3.____

4.____

5. The one of the following which is the MAJOR cause of employee lateness is

   A. low morale
   B. excessive fatigue
   C. accidents
   D. sickness

6. For officers to work together smoothly, teamwork is necessary.
   Which one of the following statements BEST describes the relationship between leadership and teamwork?

   A. Leadership cannot exist without teamwork.
   B. Teamwork cannot exist without leadership.
   C. Leadership and teamwork are one and the same.
   D. There is no relationship between leadership and teamwork.

7. For superiors who wish to achieve proper discipline among subordinates, it is generally MOST difficult to

   A. obtain rapid compliance with orders and directives
   B. prevent subordinates from questioning orders that are issued to them
   C. achieve compliance with orders while encouraging individual initiative
   D. use punishment to prevent infractions of the rules

8. Of the following, it is MOST likely that laxity in administering discipline will result in

   A. a loss of respect for their superior on the part of subordinates
   B. the satisfactory completion of the organization's job
   C. an increase in the number of disturbances at centers
   D. the establishment of proper conditions for successful administration

9. In dealing with a subordinate who shows a lack of interest in performing his duties, a superior officer should GENERALLY

   A. assign to him all the difficult work
   B. give him more responsibility
   C. inspect his performance more often than usual
   D. give him direct, detailed orders

10. A superior officer who has a highly motivated group of officers under his command GENERALLY

    A. shows an interest in how they are doing and is willing to back them up
    B. spends most of his time in closely supervising his subordinates
    C. supervises mainly through one of his subordinate officers
    D. is management-oriented rather than subordinate-oriented

11. As a superior, you might have to supervise subordinate officers who are very enthusiastic and ambitious.
    Which one of the following is the BEST reason for carefully watching the work of such officers?
    They

    A. may produce so much work that other officers resent them
    B. may appear to be overly concerned about being promoted
    C. might make decisions before obtaining the necessary information
    D. may be seeking the superior's job

12. In dealing with the public, officers should behave with courtesy.
    Which one of the following practices would be LEAST effective in promoting courtesy?

    A. Giving advice on subjects about which you are not well informed
    B. Learning to take constructive criticism intelligently
    C. Avoiding discussions of a personal nature
    D. Treating members of the public as you would like to be treated

13. When directing the officers under your command, which one of the following is generally the MOST effective method of supervision?

    A. Provide your directions through written orders to prevent misunderstanding
    B. Supervise every detail of the work closely so that it is carried out exactly as you want it
    C. Limit your concern to getting the job done and not to the people doing the work
    D. Set up general standards and goals so that officers have leeway as to how to achieve them

14. Leadership is particularly important in the security field.
    Of the following, people GENERALLY expect their leader to

    A. state, *Do as I say, not as I do*
    B. refuse to allow changes in orders
    C. get many of his ideas from his subordinates
    D. take his feelings out on those who make mistakes

15. The MOST important single factor in the selection of a person for assignment to a position of greater responsibility should be his

    A. demonstrated ability to do the job
    B. schooling, both civilian and military
    C. training and experience on the job
    D. length of service

16. Security training received by security officers and noted in their personnel charts or records should NOT be used as a basis for

    A. indicating individual degrees of skill
    B. assigning officers to particular shifts
    C. establishing priorities of instruction
    D. presenting a consolidated picture of the training status

17. As a superior officer, you note that one of your subordinates has not been performing his job properly. You discover that the cause of this problem seems to be that he drinks excessively when off duty.
    Of the following, the BEST way to handle this situation is to

    A. discipline the officer to the fullest extent possible
    B. discuss the problem and possible solutions with the officer's fellow workers
    C. wait until the officer has straightened himself out and then counsel him
    D. have a blunt and firm talk with the officer and direct him to seek treatment

18. Officers who are overly sensitive to criticism are one of the problems that superiors must deal with.
Of the following, which is the BEST way to handle such officers?
They should

   A. not be talked to differently from other officers
   B. be criticized only on serious mistakes
   C. not be criticized at all
   D. be reassured of their worth to their unit

19. A superior officer who suspects an employee of petty office theft calls the employee to his office and questions him directly.
In this situation, the superior's action is

   A. *desirable,* primarily because the subordinate should be allowed to answer these accusations privately
   B. *desirable,* primarily because confrontation will persuade the employee to tell the truth
   C. *undesirable,* primarily because line department personnel should handle such matters
   D. *undesirable,* primarily because direct confrontation might unnecessarily embarrass the employee

20. Assume that a certain superior officer assigns a task, without explanation, to a new subordinate who is not yet accepted by the work group.
Of the following, the MOST likely result of this action would be to

   A. encourage the subordinate to perform at his best
   B. make the subordinate feel insecure about proving himself
   C. stimulate other officers to do their best to impress the new staff member
   D. cause the experienced officers to feel inferior

21. A newly appointed superior officer often faces the problem of supervising officers who were formerly close personal friends of his.
In this situation, the one of the following which is the BEST approach to take toward these officers is to

   A. break all ties with former friends
   B. stay personally close with friends as this is always an advantage on the job
   C. maintain a relationship of easy, occasional familiarity
   D. become businesslike on the job but remain close socially

22. Assume that you, as a superior officer, are talking over a proposed change in procedure with your subordinates which would require their full cooperation.
Which one of the following actions would be MOST appropriate for you to take if your subordinates suggest modifications in the procedure?

   A. Prepare arguments against your subordinates' suggestions while you are listening to them
   B. Refuse to accept suggestions for changes since procedures can't be modified
   C. Listen carefully since your subordinates' suggestions may have merit
   D. Accept the recommendations of your more experienced subordinates

23. The successful supervisor should be aware that two of his most important assets are patience and understanding.
Of the following actions by a supervisor, the one that is LEAST likely to demonstrate these qualities would be to

    A. make deadlines realistic and reachable
    B. reprimand an employee the minute he makes a mistake
    C. assist employees in work-related problems
    D. discuss changes in procedures with subordinates

23.____

24. One of a supervisor's goals should be to create and maintain a force of loyal subordinates with high morale. This objective is likely to be achieved by all of the following EXCEPT

    A. making subordinate officers feel that their job is an important one
    B. encouraging supervisors to be concerned with the individual needs of subordinates
    C. giving subordinate officers an opportunity to express their thoughts, likes, and interests to their supervisors
    D. having supervisors rely only on the advice of trusted employees when resolving disputes between subordinates

24.____

25. One of a supervisor's major responsibilities is to evaluate the performance of his subordinates.
Which one of the following practices would be LEAST productive in developing meaningful evaluations from performance interviews?

    A. Make positive statements only
    B. Outline the points to discuss
    C. Adjust to the individual and situation
    D. Allow the employee to participate

25.____

KEY (CORRECT ANSWERS)

1.	C	11.	C
2.	C	12.	A
3.	C	13.	D
4.	B	14.	C
5.	A	15.	A
6.	B	16.	B
7.	C	17.	D
8.	A	18.	D
9.	B	19.	A
10.	A	20.	B

21. C
22. C
23. B
24. D
25. A

TEST 2

DIRECTIONS: Each question or incomplete statement is followed by several suggested answers or completions. Select the one that BEST answers the question or completes the statement. *PRINT THE LETTER OF THE COREECT ANSWER IN THE SPACE AT THE RIGHT.*

1. Assume that you are a superior officer concerned with improving the attitude of your subordinates toward their work.
Of the following, the action that is MOST likely to improve this attitude would be for you to

    A. allow your subordinates to take extra time off
    B. interpret rules and regulations leniently
    C. request a merit increase in salary for your subordinates
    D. train your subordinates to perform at the highest possible level

    1.____

2. Assume that two of the officers under your command are hotly disputing the accuracy of a log book entry. One of the officers asks for your opinion.
Which of the following would be LEAST advisable for you to do in this situation?

    A. Ask the officers to present their views calmly
    B. Keep your temper and remain impartial
    C. Stop the argument and then give your decision
    D. Judge the argument in proportion to its importance

    2.____

3. A superior officer notices that one of his subordinates is not doing his job.
In this situation, it would be MOST appropriate for the superior officer to

    A. caution the subordinate officer promptly
    B. ignore the incident this time
    C. check on the subordinate officer's behavior in an hour
    D. warn the subordinate officer at the end of his work day that a report may be filed

    3.____

4. A recently appointed superior officer finds it difficult to make the decisions required in his new position.
Which one of the following suggestions would be MOST helpful to him in overcoming this problem?

    A. Don't be concerned because everyone makes mistakes, and any mistake caused by your decisions will be ignored.
    B. Remember that you will be judged by the long-range soundness of all of your decisions.
    C. Since you are now in charge of a number of officers, let them bear the decision-making responsibility.
    D. Remember that you have a superior and that he can make the decision for you.

    4.____

5. Of the following, the BEST reason for a superior officer to nake inspections and rounds is to

    A. observe the physical appearance of personnel
    B. determine whether communication equipment is working properly

    5.____

C. decide whether adequate records are being kept
D. see that the performance of subordinates conforms with departmental standards

6. Assume that you, as a superior officer, have made an inspection and have submitted recommendations for improvements.
Which one of the following actions should be taken to assure that the desired results are obtained from the inspection?
You should

   A. distribute copies of the recommendations to all members of the force
   B. follow-up to determine whether the recommended improvements have been made
   C. give credit to other officers when it is due in order to help increase morale
   D. set up a schedule so that you inspect once a week

7. Assume that you have noticed that one of your subordinates has been quiet and rather depressed for two to three days with no change in his usual satisfactory job performance.
Of the following, the BEST action for you to take in this situation is to

   A. ask him to describe his feelings in detail
   B. act as if you noticed no change in the subordinate's behavior
   C. tell him to forget what's bothering him
   D. recommend that he seek professional guidance

8. Assume that you wish to introduce a change in your subordinates' work procedures in order to improve their performance.
Of the following, the BEST way to gain acceptance of this change is for you to

   A. stress its positive aspects
   B. downgrade past practices
   C. delay discussing it for a while
   D. order your subordinates to follow the new procedure at once

9. Suppose you come across two of your subordinate officers having an argument about the boundaries of their patrol posts.
Which of the following is the LEAST advisable course of action for you to take after stopping the argument?

   A. Tell the officers to speak with you individually
   B. Have the officers submit their views in writing for you to evaluate properly when you have time
   C. Meet with both officers in your office after they finish their tours
   D. Tell the officers to consult you on such matters in the future

10. Assume that a superior officer is explaining a new rule to his men at roll call. One officer states that he does not like the rule. The superior tells the officer that he agrees with him, but that the rule must be followed anyway. In this situation, the superior officer's statement was

    A. *proper*, chiefly because the men should know where superiors stand on rules and regulations
    B. *improper*, chiefly because superiors should not indicate disagreement with a change in rules since they must enforce them

C. *proper,* chiefly because efficiency improves when supervisors and subordinates agree on new rules
D. *improper,* chiefly because questions regarding rule changes should be answered at staff meetings rather than at roll call

11. Assume that you find that several of your subordinate officers have not performed satisfactorily during the last few emergency situations at your work location. The one of the following actions which is LEAST likely to improve their performance is for you to

    A. keep the subordinates informed about how they performed after each emergency
    B. stay alert for officers who are having difficulty with their work
    C. circulate among the officers at emergencies
    D. avoid the use of criticism

11.____

12. Of the following qualifications for an officer, the one that is MOST important is the ability to

    A. understand and get along with people
    B. write a good report
    C. overcome resistance to arrest
    D. solve crimes

12.____

13. Assume that you have noticed that one of your subordinate officers makes errors when questioning clients. You discuss with him the proper method to use when questioning clients.
Of the following, your NEXT step should be to

    A. ask another officer to check on your subordinate's procedure when questioning clients
    B. tell the officer to discuss with others how they question clients
    C. have the officer report regularly to you about the clients he questions
    D. watch the officer to see how he questions clients

13.____

14. One of the MOST important rules to follow when communicating with your superior is:

    A. Report everything that happens at your work location to him
    B. Pass on to him rumors and gossip heard within your center
    C. Let him hear from you first about any unusual success, problem or error
    D. Assign to one of your subordinates the responsibility of communicating with your supervisor

14.____

15. A superior officer may be required to instruct subordinates in the performance of their tasks.
Which of the following would NOT be proper when instructing a small group of employees?

    A. Use simple language
    B. Explain the procedure and the reason for the procedure
    C. Demonstrate one step at a time
    D. Use the lecture method instead of the discussion method whenever possible

15.____

4 (#2)

16. Assume that a new officer has joined your unit. Which of the following approaches should you, as his superior officer, use in introducing him to the job?   16.____

    A. Put him right to work; he will learn best through his mistakes
    B. Act sternly, thereby gaining his respect and indicating the proper supervisor-subordinate relationship
    C. Give him the overall picture of the department and unit he is in
    D. Praise him, even when he makes errors, in order to gain his confidence

17. When a new officer begins work, he will often perform tasks ineffectively, thus requiring corrective action by his supervisor.
    In this situation, which one of the following represents the MOST desirable course of action for the supervisor?   17.____

    A. Point out specific errors in performance and how to correct them
    B. Tell the new officer that he is not doing the job properly and assign him to a new task
    C. Avoid criticism in the beginning since it may result in bitterness
    D. Do not criticize because criticism is not currently considered an acceptable tool of management

18. Of the following types of work, the one that is MOST likely to lead to dissatisfaction is work that is   18.____

    A. difficult to perform   B. tiring to complete
    C. uncomplicated   D. unimportant

19. When instructing subordinates to perform new tasks, the one of the following that is LEAST important in helping then to learn is to   19.____

    A. explain the procedure to them in a step-by-step manner
    B. show them what they must do
    C. let them do the task under guidance
    D. have them perform the task without supervision so they may learn from their mistakes

20. Which one of the following is the MOST important single thing to bear in mind about giving orders?   20.____

    A. An order should be given to a capable employee, not an uncooperative one.
    B. If an order is given correctly, you will not have to check the work.
    C. An order should be given in as forceful a manner as possible to assure that it is understood.
    D. An order is given because it is necessary to bring about certain results.

21. Suppose that a subordinate asks you about a rumor he has heard. The rumor deals with a subject which your superiors consider *confidential*.
    Which of the following BEST describes how you should answer the officer?
    Tell   21.____

    A. the officer that you don't make the rules and that he should speak to higher ranking officers
    B. the officer that you will ask your superior for information

C. him only that you cannot comment on the matter
D. him the rumor is not true

22. Superior officers often find it difficult to *get their message across* when instructing newly appointed officers in their various duties.
The MAIN reason for this is generally that the

   A. duties of the officers have increased
   B. superior officer is often so expert in his area that he fails to see it from the learner's point of view
   C. superior officer adapts his instruction to the slowest learner in the group
   D. new officers are younger, less concerned with job security, and more interested in fringe benefits

23. Assume that you are discussing a security problem with an officer under your command. During the discussion, you see that the officer's eyes are turning away from you and that he is not paying attention.
In order to get the officer's attention, you should FIRST

   A. ask him to look you in the eye
   B. talk to him about sports
   C. tell him he is being very rude
   D. change your tone of voice

24. As a superior officer, you may find it necessary to conduct meetings with your subordinates.
Of the following, which would be MOST helpful in assuring that a meeting accomplishes the purpose for which it was called?

   A. Give notice of the conclusions you would like to reach at the start of the meeting
   B. Delay the start of the meeting until everyone is present
   C. Write down points to be discussed in proper sequence
   D. Make sure everyone is clear on whatever conclusions have been reached and on what must be done after the meeting

25. Every superior officer will occasionally be called upon to deliver a reprimand to a subordinate. If done properly, this can greatly help an officer improve his performance.
Which one of the following is NOT a good practice to follow when giving a reprimand?

   A. Maintain your composure and temper
   B. Reprimand a subordinate in the presence of other officers so they can learn the same lesson
   C. Try to understand why the officer was not able to perform satisfactorily
   D. Let your knowledge of the officer involved determine the exact nature of the reprimand

KEY (CORRECT ANSWERS)

1.	D		11.	D
2.	C		12.	A
3.	A		13.	D
4.	B		14.	C
5.	D		15.	D
6.	B		16.	C
7.	B		17.	A
8.	A		18.	D
9.	B		19.	D
10.	B		20.	D

21. B
22. B
23. D
24. D
25. B

TEST 3

DIRECTIONS: Each question or incomplete statement is followed by several suggested answers or completions. Select the one that BEST answers the question or completes the statement. *PRINT THE LETTER OF THE CORRECT ANSWER IN THE SPACE AT THE RIGHT.*

1. Of the following, the PRIMARY purpose of communications between subordinates and superiors is to

   A. develop language skills
   B. enable subordinates to air their grievances
   C. help establish friendly ties
   D. solve job problems

   1._____

2. Of the following, the MOST necessary elements of good communication are

   A. openness and form
   B. details and subjectivity
   C. speed and dependability
   D. length and appearance

   2._____

3. Of the following, the MOST important role of a supervisor is that of

   A. being able to understand how his men feel about their assignments
   B. establishing good contacts with the administration
   C. fulfilling his responsibility to the assigned position
   D. presenting a good public image on the behalf of his organization

   3._____

4. Of the following, the LEAST desirable behavior of a senior officer would be for him to

   A. attempt to gain the respect of superiors
   B. attempt to find causes of high employee turnover
   C. ignore infrequent latenesses
   D. ignore suggestions which may prove unworthy

   4._____

5. A senior officer who consults with his subordinates about operational planning is GENERALLY

   A. attempting to prove his supervisory ability
   B. developing their job participation and cooperation
   C. passing down his responsibilities to others
   D. searching for an employee with supervisory ability

   5._____

6. If a senior officer conducted supervision and inspection programs in order to become aware of his men's conduct, he would GENERALLY be considered to be

   A. excessively strict and authoritarian
   B. looking for potential troublemakers
   C. overconscientious in his work
   D. performing a vital duty

   6._____

7. Of the following, the BEST reason for a supervisor's evaluation of his own on-the-job performance is to enable him to

   A. find the best methods of supervising his men and in getting the job done
   B. give the impression that he is sincere in trying to become a better supervisor

   7._____

C. make a favorable impression on his superiors
D. make his work seem more important than it actually is

8. Assume that you are a senior officer making a performance evaluation of an officer. The reason for NOT drawing conclusions too quickly is CHIEFLY that

   A. without due consideration of all the facts, you are likely to evaluate the officer on biased personal judgment
   B. evaluation reports take a great deal of time and thought
   C. senior officers must consult with superiors before drawing conclusions about a subordinate's performance
   D. the officer might try to disprove any wrong information which you may have obtained about him

9. A senior officer notices two officers, known to be good workers, playing practical jokes and pranks on the other employees.
In this case, disciplinary action is

   A. *desirable,* chiefly because horseplay on the job is not, strictly speaking, against the rules
   B. *undesirable,* chiefly because good workers tend to correct their own improper actions
   C. *desirable,* chiefly because horseplay could provoke other employees and that would disrupt normal work routine
   D. *undesirable,* chiefly because a supervisor should not get involved with employees' affairs

10. Resistance to or resentment of training is likely to be an attitude shown by many officers. Therefore, it is important for a senior officer to understand the causes of his men's attitudes and learn how to deal with them. Of the following, which is the BEST method of lessening an officer's resentment of training?

    A. Give the officers extra time off for taking part in the training program
    B. Openly criticize the officer who often makes mistakes during training
    C. Recommend promotions for those who complete the training program quickest
    D. Explain that the purpose of the training is to help them perform their jobs more efficiently

11. A senior officer required all officers under his supervision to submit a weekly report based on information from their daily log (memo) entries. The senior officer did not examine these reports, but he did file them as proof that the officers were not *sleeping* on the job.
In general, this practice of the senior officer is considered

    A. *correct,* chiefly because the senior officer has little need of the reports since he is usually on the scene to observe the performance of his men
    B. *incorrect,* chiefly because, if the senior officer asked for reports, he should read or use the information they contain
    C. *correct,* chiefly because any information an officer had could only be based on daily occurrences
    D. *incorrect,* chiefly because the senior officer is placing too much emphasis on accuracy of paper work

12. Selecting an employee to be trained for performing the supervisor's duties is generally considered

    A. *desirable*, chiefly because it allows the supervisor to avoid many of his duties
    B. *undesirable*, chiefly because it creates the impression that the supervisor is showing favoritism
    C. *desirable*, chiefly because supervisory coverage is assured in the absence of the supervisor
    D. *undesirable*, chiefly because the trainee will cause the supervisor to worry about possible competition and thus neglect the performance of his duties

13. When discussing lateness with an employee, a supervisor should take the employee to an area where the problem can be discussed privately
    Generally, this practice is considered

    A. *desirable,* chiefly because it gives the employee an opportunity to converse with the supervisor in a very casual way
    B. *desirable,* chiefly because it keeps the problem from being discussed in front of an audience
    C. *undesirable,* chiefly because isolating an employee from his co-workers causes the *rumor-mongers* to spread false gossip about the matter
    D. *undesirable,* chiefly because trivial matters can be mentioned in the open without any repercussions

14. When an officer shows a pattern of abuse in his use of sick leave, a senior officer should

    A. ask the officer for medical proof of all future illnesses
    B. discourage other officers from abusing sick leave by giving the offending officer a public warning
    C. interview the officer and inquire about the reasons for his behavior
    D. acknowledge the officer's right to sick leave as set forth in departmental rules and regulations

15. Of the following, the MAJOR reason why grapevines generally develop in an agency is that

    A. employees have too much idle time
    B. employees want to socialize and gossip with other employees while working
    C. superior officers avoid reporting bad news downward from management to subordinates
    D. there is a communication gap between management and employees

16. If a newly-assigned senior officer is doubtful about the exact details of the assignment he is about to give to an officer, he should GENERALLY

    A. ask to speak to the officer in private and give him another assignment
    B. delay giving the assignment until he clears up his own doubt
    C. attempt to explain to the officer what he knows about the assignment in the best possible way
    D. put the assignment in writing

17. Of the following situations, which one would justify a supervisor's giving direct orders to another supervisor's subordinate?

    A. A supervisor away from his normal assignment observes a serious disturbance and gives orders to the officers in that area.
    B. A supervisor foresees a problem that will arise the next day in another district and immediately proceeds to inform the other supervisor's officers of the action they should take.
    C. A supervisor tells an officer under another supervisor to perform a duty a week from today because he feels it is an urgent matter.
    D. None of the above situations would justify direct supervision by any senior officer.

18. In the planning process, which of the following is NOT a recommended practice in preparing your final plan of action?

    A. Obtain all important available facts related to the problem
    B. Clarify the problem before any plan is created
    C. Make the plan easy to understand so that it can be carried out efficiently
    D. Never make assumptions or forecasts about what could occur

19. Of the following, the BEST way for a senior officer to get his subordinates to carry out his orders is to

    A. explain whenever possible why the orders are being given
    B. let subordinates know in advance the penalties for disobeying his orders
    C. describe the steps that must be followed in performing each order
    D. issue all orders in the form of direct and positive commands

20. It is MOST correct to state that race prejudice is to the GREATEST extent

    A. an inborn human characteristic
    B. the result of training and group association
    C. the product of ghetto areas
    D. a condition limited to adults only

21. *Scapegoating* is a form of prejudice which results MAINLY from

    A. degrading minority groups in an effort to secure status for one's own group
    B. shifting the blame for social inadequacies and ills from oneself to others
    C. thinking of people not as individual persons but rather placing them in carelessly formed, all-embracing classifications
    D. maintaining the existing order to prevent other groups from rising in social and economic status

22. The MOST important step in democratic supervision is

    A. allowing the employee a chance to apologize whenever he makes an error
    B. keeping tight control over employees
    C. making the employee realize that he needs your approval in order to keep his position
    D. showing an interest in the welfare of the employee

23. Evaluating a subordinate's likes and dislikes concerning his work is GENERALLY considered to be

   A. valuable in assigning work details to the subordinate
   B. necessary only when the subordinate complains of dissatisfaction with his daily duties
   C. unnecessary and a waste of time
   D. useful only in establishing a good relationship with the subordinate

24. Employee motivation is very critical in keeping up the morale of employees.
Of the following, which is generally the BEST method of supervision which both motivates and maintains high morale?

   A. Aid employees in finding satisfaction in their assignments even if it requires extra time and responsibility
   B. Allow employees to work with a free hand and without daily interruptions
   C. Don't get involved or become concerned with interests or problems of employees outside the job
   D. Prove your friendship to a select number of employees so that the remainder of the staff will feel you are a *good guy* to work for

25. When attempting to motivate an experienced individual, it is BEST for a senior officer to appeal to the person's

   A. emotions   B. positive interests
   C. negative feelings   D. inhibitions

KEY (CORRECT ANSWERS)

1.	D		11.	B
2.	C		12.	C
3.	C		13.	B
4.	D		14.	C
5.	B		15.	D
6.	D		16.	B
7.	A		17.	A
8.	A		18.	D
9.	C		19.	A
10.	D		20.	B

21. B
22. D
23. A
24. A
25. B

REPORT WRITING
EXAMINATION SECTION
TEST 1

DIRECTIONS: Each question or incomplete statement is followed by several suggested answers or completions. Select the one that BEST answers the question or completes the statement. *PRINT THE LETTER OF THE CORRECT ANSWER IN THE SPACE AT THE RIGHT.*

Questions 1-3.

DIRECTIONS: Questions 1 to 3 are based on the following example of a report. The report consists of ten numbered sentences, some of which are *not* consistent with the principles of good report writing.

(1) On the evening of February 24, Roscoe and Leroy, two members of the "Red Devils," were entering with a bottle of wine in their hands. (2) It was unusually good wine for these boys to buy, (3) I told them to give me the bottle and they refused, and added that they wouldn"t let anyone "put them out." (4) I told them they were entitled to have a good time, but they could not do it the way they wanted; there were certain rules they had to observe, (5) At this point, Roscoe said he had seen me box at camp and suggested that Leroy not accept my offer. (6) Then I said firmly that the admission fee did not give them the authority to tell me what to do. (7) I also told them that, if they thought I would fight them over such a matter, they were sadly mistaken. (8) I added, however, that we could go to the gym right now and settle it another way if they wished. (9) Leroy immediately said that he was sorry, he had not understood the rules, and he did not want his quarter back. (10) On the other hand, they would not give up their bottle either, so they left the premises..

1. Only material that is relevant to the main thought of a report should be included. Which of the following sentences from the report contains material which is LEAST relevant to this report? Sentence

   A. 2 B. 3 C. 8 D. 9

2. A good report should be arranged in logical order. Which of the following sentences from the report does NOT appear in its proper sequence in the report? Sentence

   A. 3 B. 5 C. 7 D. 9

3. Reports should include all essential information.
   Of the following, the MOST important fact that is *missing* from this report is:

   A. Who was involved in the incident
   B. How the incident was resolved
   C. When the incident took place
   D. Where the incident took place

1.____

2.____

3.____

4. The MOST serious of the following faults *commonly* found in explanatory reports is

   A. the use of slang terms
   B. excessive details
   C. C. personal bias
   D. redundancy

5. In reviewing a report he has prepared to submit to his superiors, a supervisor finds that his paragraphs are a typewritten page long and decides to make some revisions.
   Of the following, the MOST important question he should ask about each paragraph is:

   A. Are the words too lengthy?
   B. Is the idea under discussion too abstract?
   C. Is more than one central thought being expressed?
   D. Are the sentences too long?

6. The summary or findings of a long management report intended for the typical manager should, *generally,* appear

   A. at the very beginning of the report
   B. at the end of the report
   C. throughout the report
   D. in the middle of the report

7. In preparing a report that includes several tables, if not otherwise instructed, the typist should *most properly* include a list of tables

   A. in the introductory part of the report
   B. at the end of each chapter in the body of the report
   C. in the supplementary part of the report as an appendix
   D. in the supplementary part of the report as a part of the index

8. When typing a preliminary draft of a report, the one of the following which you should *generally* NOT do is to

   A. erase typing errors and deletions rather than "X"ing them out
   B. leave plenty of room at the top, bottom and sides of each page
   C. make only the number of copies that you are asked to make
   D. type double or triple space

9. When you determine the methods of emphasis you will use in typing the titles, headings and subheadings of a report, the one of the following which it is MOST important to keep in mind is that

   A. all headings of the same rank should be typed in the same way
   B. all headings should be typed in the single style which is most pleasing to the eye
   C. headings should not take up more than one third of the page width
   D. only one method should be used for all headings, whatever their rank

10. The one of the following ways in which inter-office memoranda *differ* from long formal reports is that they, *generally,*

    A. are written as if the reader is familiar with the vocabulary and technical background of the writer
    B. do not have a "subject line" which describes the major topic covered in the text

C. include a listing of reference materials which support the memo writer's conclusions
D. require that a letter of transmittal be attached

11. It is *preferable* to print information on a field report rather than write it out longhand MAINLY because

    A. printing takes less time to write than writing longhand
    B. printing is usually easier to read than longhand writing
    C. longhand writing on field reports is not acceptable in court cases
    D. printing occupies less space on a report than longhand writing

12. Of the following characteristics of a written report, the one that is MOST important is its

    A. length   B. accuracy   C. organization   D. grammar

13. A written report to your superior contains many spelling errors.
    Of the following statements relating to spelling errors, the one that is *most nearly* correct is that

    A. this is unimportant as long as the meaning of the report is clear
    B. readers of the report will ignore the many spelling errors
    C. readers of the report will get a poor opinion of the writer of the report
    D. spelling errors are unimportant as long as the grammar is correct

14. Written reports to your superior should have the same general arrangement and layout. The BEST reason for this requirement is that the

    A. report will be more accurate
    B. report will be more complete
    C. person who reads the report will know what the subject of the report is
    D. person who reads the report will know where to look for information in the report

15. The first paragraph of a report usually contains detailed information on the subject of the report.
    Of the following, the BEST reason for this requirement is to enable the

    A. reader to quickly find the subject of the report
    B. typist to immediately determine the subject of the report so that she will understand what she is typing
    C. clerk to determine to whom copies of the report shall be routed
    D. typist to quickly determine how many copies of the report will be needed

16. Of the following statements concerning reports, the one which is LEAST valid is:

    A. A case report should contain factual material to support conclusions made.
    B. An extremely detailed report may be of less value than a brief report giving the essential facts.
    C. Highly technical language should be avoided as far as possible in preparing a report to be used at a court trial.
    D. The position of the important facts in a report does not influence the emphasis placed on them by the reader.

17. Suppose that you realize that you have made an error in a report that has been forwarded to another unit. You know that this error is not likely to be discovered for some time.
Of the following, the MOST advisable course of action for you to take is to

    A. approach the supervisor of the other unit on an informal basis, and ask him to correct the error
    B. say nothing about it since most likely one error will not invalidate the entire report
    C. tell your supervisor immediately that you have made an error so that it may be corrected, if necessary
    D. wait until the error is discovered and then admit that you had made it

18. In a report, words in a sentence must be arranged properly to make sure that the intended meaning of the sentence is clear.
The sentence below that does NOT make sense because a clause has been separated from the word on which its meaning depends is:

    A. To be a good writer, clarity is necessary.
    B. To be a good writer, you must write clearly.
    C. You must write clearly to be a good writer.
    D. Clarity is necessary to good writing.

19. The use of a graph to show statistical data in a report is *superior* to a table because it

    A. emphasizes approximations
    B. emphasizes facts and relationships more dramatically
    C. presents data more accurately
    D. is easily understood by the average reader

20. Of the following, the degree of formality required of a written report is, *most likely* to depend on the

    A. subject matter of the report
    B. frequency of its occurrence
    C. amount of time available for its preparation
    D. audience for whom the report is intended

Questions 21-25.

DIRECTIONS: Questions 21 through 25 consist of sets of four sentences lettered A, B, C, and For each question, choose the sentence which is grammatically and stylistically *most appropriate* for use in a *formal* WRITTEN REPORT.

21. A. It is recommended, therefore, that the impasse panelhearings are to be convened on September 30.
    B. It is therefore recommended that the impasse panel hearings be convened on September 30.
    C. Therefore, it is recommended to convene the impasse panel hearings on September 30.
    D. It is recommended that the impasse panel hearings therefore should be convened on September 30.

22. A. Penalties have been assessed for violating the TaylorLaw by several unions.
    B. When they violated provisions of the Taylor Law, several unions were later penalized.
    C. Several unions have been penalized for violating provisions of the Taylor Law.
    D. Several unions' violating provisions of the Taylor Law resulted in them being penalized.

    22.____

23. A. The number of disputes settled through mediation has increased significantly over the past two years.
    B. The number of disputes settled through mediation are increasing significantly over two-year periods.
    C. Over the past two years, through mediation, the number of disputes settled increased significantly.
    D. There is a significant increase over the past two years of the number of disputes settled through mediation.

    23.____

24. A. The union members will vote to determine if the contract is to be approved.
    B. It is not yet known whether the union members will ratify the proposed contract.
    C. When the union members vote, that will determine the new contract.
    D. Whether the union members will ratify the proposed contract, it is not yet known.

    24.____

25. A. The parties agreed to an increase in fringe benefits in return for greater work productivity.
    B. Greater productivity was agreed to be provided in return for increased fringe benefits.
    C. Productivity and fringe benefits are interrelated; the higher the former, the more the latter grows.
    D. The contract now provides that the amount of fringe benefits will depend upon the level of output by the workers.

    25.____

KEY (CORRECT ANSWERS)

1.	A	11.	B
2.	B	12.	B
3.	D	13.	C
4.	C	14.	D
5.	C	15.	A
6.	A	16.	D
7.	A	17.	C
8.	A	18.	A
9.	A	19.	B
10.	A	20.	D

21. B
22. C
23. A
24. B
25. A

———

TEST 2

Questions 1-4.

DIRECTIONS: Answer Questions 1 through 4 on the basis of the following report which was prepared by a supervisor for inclusion in his agency's annual report.

Line #

1   On Oct. 13, I was assigned to study the salaries paid
2   to clerical employees in various titles by the city and by
3   private industry in the area.
4   In order to get the data I needed, I called Mr. Johnson at
5   the Bureau of the Budget and the payroll officers at X Corp.—
6   a brokerage house, Y Co.—an insurance company, and Z Inc.—
7   a publishing firm. None of them was available and I had to call
8   all of them again the next day.
9   When I finally got the information I needed, I drew up a
10 chart, which is attached. Note that not all of the companies I
11 contacted employed people at all the different levels used in the
12 city service.
13 The conclusions I draw from analyzing this information is
14 as follows: The city's entry-level salary is about average for
15 the region; middle-level salaries are generally higher in the
16 city government than in private industry; but salaries at the
17 highest levels in private industry are better than city em-
18 ployees' pay.

1. Which of the following criticisms about the style in which this report is written is MOST valid?   1.____

   A. It is too informal.   B. It is too concise.
   C. It is too choppy.   D. The syntax is too complex.

2. Judging from the statements made in the report, the method followed by this employee in performing his research was   2.____

   A. *good;* he contacted a representative sample of businesses in the area
   B. *poor;* he should have drawn more definite conclusions
   C. *good;* he was persistent in collecting information
   D. *poor;* he did not make a thorough study

3. One sentence in this report contains a grammatical error. This sentence *begins* on line number   3.____

   A. 4   B. 7   C. 10   D. 13

4. The type of information given in this report which should be presented in footnotes or in an appendix, is the   4.____

A. purpose of the study
B. specifics about the businesses contacted
C. reference to the chart
D. conclusions drawn by the author

5. Of the following, a DISTINGUISHING characteristic of a written report intended for the head of your agency as compared to a report prepared for a lower-echelon staff member is that the report for the agency head should, *usually,* include

    A. considerably more detail, especially statistical data
    B. the essential details in an abbreviated form
    C. all available source material
    D. an annotated bibliography

6. Assume that you are asked to write a lengthy report for use by the administrator of your agency, the subject of which is "The Impact of Proposed New Data Processing Operations on Line Personnel" in your agency. You decide that the *most appropriate* type of report for you to prepare is an analytical report, including recommendations.
The MAIN reason for your decision is that

    A. the subject of the report is extremely complex
    B. large sums of money are involved
    C. the report is being prepared for the administrator
    D. you intend to include charts and graphs

7. Assume that you are preparing a report based on a survey dealing with the attitudes of employees in Division X regarding proposed new changes in compensating employees for working overtime. Three percent of the respondents to the survey voluntarily offer an unfavorable opinion on the method of assigning overtime work, a question not speci-cally asked of the employees.
On the basis of this information, the MOST appropriate and significant of the following comments for you to make in the report with regard to employees' attitudes on assigning overtime work is that

    A. an insignificant percentage of employees dislike the method of assigning overtime work
    B. three percent of the employees in Division X dislike the method of assigning overtime work
    C. three percent of the sample selected for the survey voiced an unfavorable opinion on the method of assigning overtime work
    D. some employees voluntarily voiced negative feelings about the method of assigning overtime work, making it impossible to determine the extent of this attitude

8. Assume that you have been asked to prepare a narrative summary of the monthly reports submitted by employees in your division.
In preparing your summary of this month's reports, the FIRST step to take is to

    A. read through the reports, noting their general content and any unusual features
    B. decide how many typewritten pages your summary should contain
    C. make a written summary of each separate report, so that you will not have to go back to the original reports again
    D. ask each employee which points he would prefer to see emphasized in your summary

9. Assume that an administrative officer is writing a brief report to his superior outlining the advantages of matrix organization. Of the following, it would be INCORRECT to state that

   A. in matrix organization, a project is emphasized by designating one individual as the focal point for all matters pertaining to it
   B. utilization of manpower can be flexible in matrix organization because a reservoir of specialists is maintained in the line operations
   C. the usual line-staff management is generally reversed in matrix organization
   D. in matrix organization, responsiveness to project needs is generally faster due to establishing needed communication lines and decision points

10. Written reports dealing with inspections of work and installations SHOULD be

    A. as long and detailed as practicable
    B. phrased with personal interpretations
    C. limited to the important facts of the inspection
    D. technically phrased to create an impression on superiors

11. It is important to use definite, exact words in preparing a descriptive report and to avoid, as much as possible, nouns that have vague meanings and, possibly, a different meaning for the reader than for the author.
    Which of the following sentences contains only nouns that are *definite* and *exact*?

    A. The free enterprise system should be vigorously encouraged in the United States.
    B. Arley Swopes climbed Mount Everest three times last year.
    C. Beauty is a characteristic of all the women at the party.
    D. Gil Noble asserts that he is a real democrat.

12. One way of shortening an unnecessarily long report is to reduce sentence length by eliminating the use of several words where a single one that does not alter the meaning will do.
    Which of the following sentences CANNOT be shortened without losing some of its information content?

    A. After being polished, the steel ball bearings ran at maximum speed.
    B. After the close of the war, John Taylor was made the recipient of a pension.
    C. In this day and age, you can call anyone up on the telephone.
    D. She is attractive in appearance, but she is a rather selfish person.

13. Employees are required to submit written reports of all unusual occurrences promptly. The BEST reason for such promptness is that the

    A. report may be too long if made at one's convenience
    B. employee will not be so likely to forget to make the report
    C. report will tend to be more accurate as to facts
    D. employee is likely to make a better report under pressure

14. In making a report, it is poor practice to erase information on the report in order to make a change because

    A. there may be a question of what was changed and why it was changed
    B. you are likely to erase through the paper and tear the report

C. the report will no longer look neat and presentable
D. the duplicate copies will be smudged

15. The one of the following which BEST describes a periodic report is that it

    A. provides a record of accomplishments for a given time span and a comparison with similar time spans in the past
    B. covers the progress made in a project that has been postponed
    C. integrates, summarizes, and, perhaps, interprets published data on technical or scientific material
    D. describes a decision, advocates a policy or action, and presents facts in support of the writer's position

16. The PRIMARY purpose of including pictorial illustrations in a formal report is *usually* to

    A. amplify information which has been adequately treated verbally
    B. present details that are difficult to describe verbally
    C. provide the reader with a pleasant, momentary distraction
    D. present supplementary information incidental to the main ideas developed in the report

KEY (CORRECT ANSWERS)

1.	A	6.	A
2.	D	7.	D
3.	D	8.	A
4.	B	9.	C
5.	B	10.	C

11. B
12. A
13. C
14. A
15. A
16. B

PREPARING WRITTEN MATERIAL

EXAMINATION SECTION
TEST 1

DIRECTIONS: Each question or incomplete statement is followed by several suggested answers or completions. Select the one that BEST answers the question or completes the statement. *PRINT THE LETTER OF THE CORRECT ANSWER IN THE SPACE AT THE RIGHT.*

1. The one of the following sentences which is LEAST acceptable from the viewpoint of correct usage is: 1.____

   A. The police thought the fugitive to be him.
   B. The criminals set a trap for whoever would fall into it.
   C. It is ten years ago since the fugitive fled from the city.
   D. The lecturer argued that criminals are usually cowards.
   E. The police removed four bucketfuls of earth from the scene of the crime.

2. The one of the following sentences which is LEAST acceptable from the viewpoint of correct usage is: 2.____

   A. The patrolman scrutinized the report with great care.
   B. Approaching the victim of the assault, two bruises were noticed by the patrolman.
   C. As soon as I had broken down the door, I stepped into the room.
   D. I observed the accused loitering near the building, which was closed at the time.
   E. The storekeeper complained that his neighbor was guilty of violating a local ordinance.

3. The one of the following sentences which is LEAST acceptable from the viewpoint of correct usage is: 3.____

   A. I realized immediately that he intended to assault the woman, so I disarmed him.
   B. It was apparent that Mr. Smith's explanation contained many inconsistencies.
   C. Despite the slippery condition of the street, he managed to stop the vehicle before injuring the child.
   D. Not a single one of them wish, despite the damage to property, to make a formal complaint.
   E. The body was found lying on the floor.

4. The one of the following sentences which contains NO error in usage is: 4.____

   A. After the robbers left, the proprietor stood tied in his chair for about two hours before help arrived.
   B. In the cellar I found the watchmans' hat and coat.
   C. The persons living in adjacent apartments stated that they had heard no unusual noises.
   D. Neither a knife or any firearms were found in the room.
   E. Walking down the street, the shouting of the crowd indicated that something was wrong.

5. The one of the following sentences which contains NO error in usage is:

    A. The policeman lay a firm hand on the suspect's shoulder.
    B. It is true that neither strength nor agility are the most important requirement for a good patrolman.
    C. Good citizens constantly strive to do more than merely comply the restraints imposed by society.
    D. No decision was made as to whom the prize should be awarded.
    E. Twenty years is considered a severe sentence for a felony.

6. Which of the following is NOT expressed in standard English usage?

    A. The victim reached a pay-phone booth and manages to call police headquarters.
    B. By the time the call was received, the assailant had left the scene.
    C. The victim has been a respected member of the community for the past eleven years.
    D. Although the lighting was bad and the shadows were deep, the storekeeper caught sight of the attacker.
    E. Additional street lights have since been installed, and the patrols have been strengthened.

7. Which of the following is NOT expressed in standard English usage?

    A. The judge upheld the attorney's right to question the witness about the missing glove.
    B. To be absolutely fair to all parties is the jury's chief responsibility.
    C. Having finished the report, a loud noise in the next room startled the sergeant.
    D. The witness obviously enjoyed having played a part in the proceedings.
    E. The sergeant planned to assign the case to whoever arrived first.

8. In which of the following is a word misused?

    A. As a matter of principle, the captain insisted that the suspect's partner be brought for questioning.
    B. The principle suspect had been detained at the station house for most of the day.
    C. The principal in the crime had no previous criminal record, but his closest associate had been convicted of felonies on two occasions.
    D. The interest payments had been made promptly, but the firm had been drawing upon the principal for these payments.
    E. The accused insisted that his high school principal would furnish him a character reference.

9. Which of the following statements is ambiguous?

    A. Mr. Sullivan explained why Mr. Johnson had been dismissed from his job.
    B. The storekeeper told the patrolman he had made a mistake.
    C. After waiting three hours, the patients in the doctor's office were sent home.
    D. The janitor's duties were to maintain the building in good shape and to answer tenants' complaints.
    E. The speed limit should, in my opinion, be raised to sixty miles an hour on that stretch of road.

10. In which of the following is the punctuation or capitalization faulty?

    A. The accident occurred at an intersection in the Kew Gardens section of Queens, near the bus stop.
    B. The sedan, not the convertible, was struck in the side.
    C. Before any of the patrolmen had left the police car received an important message from headquarters.
    D. The dog that had been stolen was returned to his master, John Dempsey, who lived in East Village.
    E. The letter had been sent to 12 Hillside Terrace, Rutland, Vermont 05701.

Questions 11-25.

DIRECTIONS: Questions 11 through 25 are to be answered in accordance with correct English usage; that is, standard English rather than nonstandard or substandard. Nonstandard and substandard English includes words or expressions usually classified as slang, dialect, illiterate, etc., which are not generally accepted as correct in current written communication. Standard English also requires clarity, proper punctuation and capitalization and appropriate use of words. Write the letter of the sentence NOT expressed in standard English usage in the space at the right.

11. A. There were three witnesses to the accident.
    B. At least three witnesses were found to testify for the plaintiff.
    C. Three of the witnesses who took the stand was uncertain about the defendant's competence to drive.
    D. Only three witnesses came forward to testify for the plaintiff.
    E. The three witnesses to the accident were pedestrians.

12. A. The driver had obviously drunk too many martinis before leaving for home.
    B. The boy who drowned had swum in these same waters many times before.
    C. The petty thief had stolen a bicycle from a private driveway before he was apprehended.
    D. The detectives had brung in the heroin shipment they intercepted.
    E. The passengers had never ridden in a converted bus before.

13. A. Between you and me, the new platoon plan sounds like a good idea.
    B. Money from an aunt's estate was left to his wife and he.
    C. He and I were assigned to the same patrol for the first time in two months.
    D. Either you or he should check the front door of that store.
    E. The captain himself was not sure of the witness's reliability.

14. A. The alarm had scarcely begun to ring when the explosion occurred.
    B. Before the firemen arrived on the scene, the second story had been destroyed.
    C. Because of the dense smoke and heat, the firemen could hardly approach the now-blazing structure.
    D. According to the patrolman's report, there wasn't nobody in the store when the explosion occurred.
    E. The sergeant's suggestion was not at all unsound, but no one agreed with him.

15. A. The driver and the passenger they were both found to be intoxicated.
    B. The driver and the passenger talked slowly and not too clearly.
    C. Neither the driver nor his passengers were able to give a coherent account of the accident.
    D. In a corner of the room sat the passenger, quietly dozing.
    E. The driver finally told a strange and unbelievable story, which the passenger contradicted.

16. A. Under the circumstances I decided not to continue my examination of the premises.
    B. There are many difficulties now not comparable with those existing in 1960.
    C. Friends of the accused were heard to announce that the witness had better been away on the day of the trial.
    D. The two criminals escaped in the confusion that followed the explosion.
    E. The aged man was struck by the considerateness of the patrolman's offer.

17. A. An assemblage of miscellaneous weapons lay on the table.
    B. Ample opportunities were given to the defendant to obtain counsel.
    C. The speaker often alluded to his past experience with youthful offenders in the armed forces.
    D. The sudden appearance of the truck aroused my suspicions.
    E. Her studying had a good affect on her grades in high school.

18. A. He sat down in the theater and began to watch the movie.
    B. The girl had ridden horses since she was four years old.
    C. Application was made on behalf of the prosecutor to cite the witness for contempt.
    D. The bank robber, with his two accomplices, were caught in the act.
    E. His story is simply not credible.

19. A. The angry boy said that he did not like those kind of friends.
    B. The merchant's financial condition was so precarious that he felt he must avail himself of any offer of assistance.
    C. He is apt to promise more than he can perform.
    D. Looking at the messy kitchen, the housewife felt like crying.
    E. A clerk was left in charge of the stolen property.

20. A. His wounds were aggravated by prolonged exposure to sub-freezing temperatures.
    B. The prosecutor remarked that the witness was not averse to changing his story each time he was interviewed.
    C. The crime pattern indicated that the burglars were adapt in the handling of explosives.
    D. His rigid adherence to a fixed plan brought him into renewed conflict with his subordinates.
    E. He had anticipated that the sentence would be delivered by noon.

21. A. The whole arraignment procedure is badly in need of revision.
    B. After his glasses were broken in the fight, he would of gone to the optometrist if he could.
    C. Neither Tom nor Jack brought his lunch to work.
    D. He stood aside until the quarrel was over.
    E. A statement in the psychiatrist's report disclosed that the probationer vowed to have his revenge.

    21.____

22. A. His fiery and intemperate speech to the striking employees fatally affected any chance of a future reconciliation.
    B. The wording of the statute has been variously construed.
    C. The defendant's attorney, speaking in the courtroom, called the official a demagogue who contempuously disregarded the judge's orders.
    D. The baseball game is likely to be the most exciting one this year.
    E. The mother divided the cookies among her two children.

    22.____

23. A. There was only a bed and a dresser in the dingy room.
    B. John is one of the few students that have protested the new rule.
    C. It cannot be argued that the child's testimony is negligible; it is, on the contrary, of the greatest importance.
    D. The basic criterion for clearance was so general that officials resolved any doubts in favor of dismissal.
    E. Having just returned from a long vacation, the officer found the city unbearably hot.

    23.____

24. A. The librarian ought to give more help to small children.
    B. The small boy was criticized by the teacher because he often wrote careless.
    C. It was generally doubted whether the women would permit the use of her apartment for intelligence operations.
    D. The probationer acts differently every time the officer visits him.
    E. Each of the newly appointed officers has 12 years of service.

    24.____

25. A. The North is the most industrialized region in the country.
    B. L. Patrick Gray 3d, the bureau's acting director, stated that, while "rehabilitation is fine" for some convicted criminals, "it is a useless gesture for those who resist every such effort."
    C. Careless driving, faulty mechanism, narrow or badly kept roads all play their part in causing accidents.
    D. The childrens' books were left in the bus.
    E. It was a matter of internal security; consequently, he felt no inclination to rescind his previous order.

    25.____

KEY (CORRECT ANSWERS)

1.	C		11.	C
2.	B		12.	D
3.	D		13.	B
4.	C		14.	D
5.	E		15.	A
6.	A		16.	C
7.	C		17.	E
8.	B		18.	D
9.	B		19.	A
10.	C		20.	C

21. B
22. E
23. B
24. B
25. D

TEST 2

DIRECTIONS: Each question or incomplete statement is followed by several suggested answers or completions. Select the one that BEST answers the question or completes the statement. *PRINT THE LETTER OF THE CORRECT ANSWER IN THE SPACE AT THE RIGHT.*

Questions 1-6.

DIRECTIONS: Each of Questions 1 through 6 consists of a statement which contains a word (one of those underlined) that is either incorrectly used because it is not in keeping with the meaning the quotation is evidently intended to convey, or is misspelled. There is only one INCORRECT word in each quotation. Of the four underlined words, determine if the first one should be replaced by the word lettered A, the second replaced by the word lettered B, the third replaced by the word lettered C, or the fourth replaced by the word lettered D. *PRINT THE LETTER OF THE REPLACEMENT WORD YOU HAVE SELECTED IN THE SPACE AT THE RIGHT.*

1. Whether one depends on fluorescent or artificial light or both, adequate standards should be maintained by means of systematic tests.

   A. natural
   C. established
   B. safeguards
   D. routine

2. A policeman has to be prepared to assume his knowledge as a social scientist in the community.

   A. forced
   C. philosopher
   B. role
   D. street

3. It is practically impossible to indicate whether a sentence is too long simply by measuring its length.

   A. almost   B. tell   C. very   D. guessing

4. Strong leaders are required to organize a community for delinquency prevention and for dissemination of organized crime and drug addiction.

   A. tactics   B. important   C. control   D. meetings

5. The demonstrators who were taken to the Criminal Courts building in Manhattan (because it was large enough to accommodate them), contended that the arrests were unwarrented.

   A. demonstraters
   C. accomodate
   B. Manhatten
   D. unwarranted

6. They were guaranteed a calm atmosphere, free from harrassment, which would be conducive to quiet consideration of the indictments.

   A. guarenteed
   C. harassment
   B. atmospher
   D. inditements

1.____

2.____

3.____

4.____

5.____

6.____

Questions 7-11.

DIRECTIONS: Each of Questions 7 through 11 consists of a statement containing four words in capital letters. One of these words in capital letters is not in keeping with the meaning which the statement is evidently intended to carry. The four words in capital letters in each statement are reprinted after the statement. Print the capital letter preceding the one of the four words which does MOST to spoil the true meaning of the statement in the space at the right.

7. Retirement and pension systems are essential not only to provide employees with a means of support in the future, but also to prevent longevity and CHARITABLE considerations from UPSETTING the PROMOTIONAL opportunities for RETIRED members of the career service. 7.____

   A. charitable B. upsetting
   C. promotional D. retired

8. Within each major DIVISION in a properly set up public or private organization, provision is made so that each NECESSARY activity is CARED for and lines of authority and responsibility are clear-cut and INFINITE. 8.____

   A. division B. necessary C. cared D. infinite

9. In public service, the scale of salaries paid must be INCIDENTAL to the services rendered, with due CONSIDERATION for the attraction of the desired MANPOWER and for the maintenance of a standard of living COMMENSURATE with the work to be performed. 9.____

   A. incidental B. consideration
   C. manpower D. commensurate

10. An understanding of the AIMS of an organization by the staff will AID greatly in increasing the DEMAND of the correspondence work of the office, and will to a large extent DETERMINE the nature of the correspondence. 10.____

    A. aims B. aid C. demand D. determine

11. BECAUSE the Civil Service Commission strongly feels that the MERIT system is a key factor in the MAINTENANCE of democratic government, it has adopted as one of its major DEFENSES the progressive democratization of its own procedures in dealing with candidates for positions in the public service. 11.____

    A. Because B. merit
    C. maintenance D. defenses

Questions 12-14.

DIRECTIONS: Questions 12 through 14 consist of one sentence each. Each sentence contains an incorrectly used word. First, decide which is the incorrectly used word. Then, from among the options given, decide which word, when substituted for the incorrectly used word, makes the meaning of the sentence clear.

EXAMPLE:
The U.S. national income exhibits a pattern of long term deflection.
A. reflection B. subjection
C. rejoicing D. growth

The word *deflection* in the sentence does not convey the meaning the sentence evidently intended to convey. The word *growth* (Answer D), when substituted for the word *deflection,* makes the meaning of the sentence clear. Accordingly, the answer to the question is D.

12. The study commissioned by the joint committee fell compassionately short of the mark and would have to be redone. 12.____
    A. successfully B. insignificantly
    C. experimentally D. woefully

13. He will not idly exploit any violation of the provisions of the order. 13.____
    A. tolerate B. refuse C. construe D. guard

14. The defendant refused to be virile and bitterly protested service. 14.____
    A. irked B. feasible C. docile D. credible

Questions 15-25.

DIRECTIONS: Questions 15 through 25 consist of short paragraphs. Each paragraph contains one word which is INCORRECTLY used because it is NOT in keeping with the meaning of the paragraph. Find the word in each paragraph which is INCORRECTLY used and then select as the answer the suggested word which should be substituted for the incorrectly used word.

SAMPLE QUESTION:
In determining who is to do the work in your unit, you will have to decide just who does what from day to day. One of your lowest responsibilities is to assign work so that everybody gets a fair share and that everyone can do his part well.
A. new B. old C. important D. performance

EXPLANATION:
The word which is NOT in keeping with the meaning of the paragraph is *lowest*. This is the INCORRECTLY used word. The suggested word *important* would be in keeping with the meaning of the paragraph and should be substituted for *lowest*. Therefore, the CORRECT answer is choice C.

15. If really good practice in the elimination of preventable injuries is to be achieved and held in any establishment, top management must refuse full and definite responsibility and must apply a good share of its attention to the task. 15.____
    A. accept B. avoidable C. duties D. problem

16. Recording the human face for identification is by no means the only service performed by the camera in the field of investigation. When the trial of any issue takes place, a word picture is sought to be distorted to the court of incidents, occurrences, or events which are in dispute. 16.____

A. appeals   B. description
C. portrayed   D. deranged

17. In the collection of physical evidence, it cannot be emphasized too strongly that a haphazard systematic search at the scene of the crime is vital. Nothing must be overlooked. Often the only leads in a case will come from the results of this search.   17.____

   A. important   B. investigation
   C. proof   D. thorough

18. If an investigator has reason to suspect that the witness is mentally stable, or a habitual drunkard, he should leave no stone unturned in his investigation to determine if the witness was under the influence of liquor or drugs, or was mentally unbalanced either at the time of the occurrence to which he testified or at the time of the trial.   18.____

   A. accused   B. clue   C. deranged   D. question

19. The use of records is a valuable step in crime investigation and is the main reason every department should maintain accurate reports. Crimes are not committed through the use of departmental records alone but from the use of all records, of almost every type, wherever they may be found and whenever they give any incidental information regarding the criminal.   19.____

   A. accidental   B. necessary
   C. reported   D. solved

20. In the years since passage of the Harrison Narcotic Act of 1914, making the possession of opium amphetamines illegal in most circumstances, drug use has become a subject of considerable scientific interest and investigation. There is at present a voluminous literature on drug use of various kinds.   20.____

   A. ingestion   B. derivatives
   C. addiction   D. opiates

21. Of course, the fact that criminal laws are extremely patterned in definition does not mean that the majority of persons who violate them are dealt with as criminals. Quite the contrary, for a great many forbidden acts are voluntarily engaged in within situations of privacy and go unobserved and unreported.   21.____

   A. symbolic   B. casual
   C. scientific   D. broad-gauged

22. The most punitive way to study punishment is to focus attention on the pattern of punitive action: to study how a penalty is applied, to study what is done to or taken from an offender.   22.____

   A. characteristic   B. degrading
   C. objective   D. distinguished

23. The most common forms of punishment in times past have been death, physical torture, mutilation, branding, public humiliation, fines, forfeits of property, banishment, transportation, and imprisonment. Although this list is by no means differentiated, practically every form of punishment has had several variations and applications.   23.____

   A. specific   B. simple
   C. exhaustive   D. characteristic

24. There is another important line of inference between ordinary and professional criminals, and that is the source from which they are recruited. The professional criminal seems to be drawn from legitimate employment and, in many instances, from parallel vocations or pursuits.   24._____

   A. demarcation
   B. justification
   C. superiority
   D. reference

25. He took the position that the success of the program was insidious on getting additional revenue.   25._____

   A. reputed
   B. contingent
   C. failure
   D. indeterminate

KEY (CORRECT ANSWERS)

1.	A	11.	D
2.	B	12.	D
3.	B	13.	A
4.	C	14.	C
5.	D	15.	B
6.	C	16.	A
7.	D	17.	D
8.	D	18.	C
9.	A	19.	D
10.	C	20.	B

21. D
22. C
23. C
24. A
25. B

TEST 3

DIRECTIONS: Each question or incomplete statement is followed by several suggested answers or completions. Select the one that BEST answers the question or completes the statement. *PRINT THE LETTER OF THE CORRECT ANSWER IN THE SPACE AT THE RIGHT.*

Questions 1-5.

DIRECTIONS: Question 1 through 5 are to be answered on the basis of the following:

You are a supervising officer in an investigative unit. Earlier in the day, you directed Detectives Tom Dixon and Sal Mayo to investigate a reported assault and robbery in a liquor store within your area of jurisdiction.

Detective Dixon has submitted to you a preliminary investigative report containing the following information:

- At 1630 hours on 2/20, arrived at Joe's Liquor Store at 350 SW Avenue with Detective Mayo to investigate A & R.
- At store interviewed Rob Ladd, store manager, who stated that he and Joe Brown (store owner) had been stuck up about ten minutes prior to our arrival.
- Ladd described the robbers as male whites in their late teens or early twenties. Further stated that one of the robbers displayed what appeared to be an automatic pistol as he entered the store, and said, *Give us the money or we'll kill you.* Ladd stated that Brown then reached under the counter where he kept a loaded .38 caliber pistol. Several shots followed, and Ladd threw himself to the floor.
- The robbers fled, and Ladd didn't know if any money had been taken.
- At this point, Ladd realized that Brown was unconscious on the floor and bleeding from a head wound.
- Ambulance called by Ladd, and Brown was removed by same to General Hospital.
- Personally interviewed John White, 382 Dartmouth Place, who stated he was inside store at the time of occurrence. White states that he hid behind a wine display upon hearing someone say, *Give us the money.* He then heard shots and saw two young men run from the store to a yellow car parked at the curb. White was unable to further describe auto. States the taller of the two men drove the car away while the other sat on passenger side in front.
- Recovered three spent .38 caliber bullets from premises and delivered them to Crime Lab.
- To General Hospital at 1800 hours but unable to interview Brown, who was under sedation and suffering from shock and a laceration of the head.
- Alarm #12487 transmitted for car and occupants.
- Case Active.

Based solely on the contents of the preliminary investigation submitted by Detective Dixon, select one sentence from the following groups of sentences which is MOST accurate and is grammatically correct.

1. A. Both robbers were armed.
    B. Each of the robbers were described as a male white.
    C. Neither robber was armed.
    D. Mr. Ladd stated that one of the robbers was armed.

2. A. Mr. Brown fired three shots from his revolver.
    B. Mr. Brown was shot in the head by one of the robbers.
    C. Mr. Brown suffered a gunshot wound of the head during the course of the robbery.
    D. Mr. Brown was taken to General Hospital by ambulance.

3. A. Shots were fired after one of the robbers said, *Give us* the money or we'll kill you.
    B. After one of the robbers demanded the money from Mr. Brown, he fired a shot.
    C. The preliminary investigation indicated that although Mr. Brown did not have a license for the gun, he was justified in using deadly physical force.
    D. Mr. Brown was interviewed at General Hospital.

4. A. Each of the witnesses were customers in the store at the time of occurrence.
    B. Neither of the witnesses interviewed was the owner of the liquor store.
    C. Neither of the witnesses interviewed were the owner of the store.
    D. Neither of the witnesses was employed by Mr. Brown.

5. A. Mr. Brown arrived at General Hospital at about 5:00 P.M.
    B. Neither of the robbers was injured during the robbery.
    C. The robbery occurred at 3:30 P.M. on February 10.
    D. One of the witnesses called the ambulance.

Questions 6-10.

DIRECTIONS: Each of Questions 6 through 10 consists of information given in outline form and four sentences labelled A, B, C, and D. For each question, choose the one sentence which CORRECTLY expresses the information given in outline form and which also displays PROPER English usage.

6. Client's Name - Joanna Jones
    Number of Children - 3
    Client's Income - None
    Client's Marital Status - Single

    A. Joanna Jones is an unmarried client with three children who have no income.
    B. Joanna Jones, who is single and has no income, a client she has three children.
    C. Joanna Jones, whose three children are clients, is single and has no income.
    D. Joanna Jones, who has three children, is an unmarried client with no income.

7. Client's Name - Bertha Smith
    Number of Children - 2
    Client's Rent - $105 per month
    Number of Rooms - 4

A. Bertha Smith, a client, pays $105 per month for her four rooms with two children.
   B. Client Bertha Smith has two children and pays $105 per month for four rooms.
   C. Client Bertha Smith is paying $105 per month for two children with four rooms.
   D. For four rooms and two children client Bertha Smith pays $105 per month.

8. Name of Employee - Cynthia Dawes
   Number of Cases Assigned - 9
   Date Cases were Assigned - 12/16
   Number of Assigned Cases Completed - 8

   A. On December 16, employee Cynthia Dawes was assigned nine cases; she has completed eight of these cases.
   B. Cynthia Dawes, employee on December 16, assigned nine cases, completed eight.
   C. Being employed on December 16, Cynthia Dawes completed eight of nine assigned cases.
   D. Employee Cynthia Dawes, she was assigned nine cases and completed eight, on December 16.

8._____

9. Place of Audit - Broadway Center
   Names of Auditors - Paul Cahn, Raymond Perez
   Date of Audit - 11/20
   Number of Cases Audited - 41

   A. On November 20, at the Broadway Center 41 cases was audited by auditors Paul Cahn and Raymond Perez.
   B. Auditors Raymond Perez and Paul Cahn has audited 41 cases at the Broadway Center on November 20.
   C. At the Broadway Center, on November 20, auditors Paul Cahn and Raymond Perez audited 41 cases.
   D. Auditors Paul Cahn and Raymond Perez at the Broadway Center, on November 20, is auditing 41 cases.

9._____

10. Name of Client - Barbra Levine
    Client's Monthly Income - $210
    Client's Monthly Expenses - $452

    A. Barbra Levine is a client, her monthly income is $210 and her monthly expenses is $452.
    B. Barbra Levine's monthly income is $210 and she is a client, with whose monthly expenses are $452.
    C. Barbra Levine is a client whose monthly income is $210 and whose monthly expenses are $452.
    D. Barbra Levine, a client, is with a monthly income which is $210 and monthly expenses which are $452.

10._____

Questions 11-13.

DIRECTIONS: Questions 11 through 13 involve several statements of fact presented in a very simple way. These statements of fact are followed by 4 choices which attempt to incorporate all of the facts into one logical sentence which is properly constructed and grammatically correct.

11.
- I. Mr. Brown was sweeping the sidewalk in front of his house.
- II. He was sweeping it because it was dirty.
- III. He swept the refuse into the street
- IV. Police Officer Green gave him a ticket.

Which one of the following BEST presents the information given above?

- A. Because his sidewalk was dirty, Mr. Brown received a ticket from Officer Green when he swept the refuse into the street.
- B. Police Officer Green gave Mr. Brown a ticket because his sidewalk was dirty and he swept the refuse into the street.
- C. Police Officer Green gave Mr. Brown a ticket for sweeping refuse into the street because his sidewalk was dirty.
- D. Mr. Brown, who was sweeping refuse from his dirty sidewalk into the street, was given a ticket by Police Officer Green.

11.____

12.
- I. Sergeant Smith radioed for help.
- II. The sergeant did so because the crowd was getting larger.
- III. It was 10:00 A.M. when he made his call.
- IV. Sergeant Smith was not in uniform at the time of occurrence.

Which one of the following BEST presents the information given above?

- A. Sergeant Smith, although not on duty at the time, radioed for help at 10 o'clock because the crowd was getting uglier.
- B. Although not in uniform, Sergeant Smith called for help at 10:00 A.M. because the crowd was getting uglier.
- C. Sergeant Smith radioed for help at 10:00 A.M. because the crowd was getting larger.
- D. Although he was not in uniform, Sergeant Smith radioed for help at 10:00 A.M. because the crowd was getting larger.

12.____

13.
- I. The payroll office is open on Fridays.
- II. Paychecks are distributed from 9:00 A.M. to 12 Noon.
- III. The office is open on Fridays because that's the only day the payroll staff is available.
- IV. It is open for the specified hours in order to permit employees to cash checks at the bank during lunch hour.

The choice below which MOST clearly and accurately presents the above idea is:

- A. Because the payroll office is open on Fridays from 9:00 A.M. to 12 Noon, employees can cash their checks when the payroll staff is available.
- B. Because the payroll staff is only available on Fridays until noon, employees can cash their checks during their lunch hour.
- C. Because the payroll staff is available only on Fridays, the office is open from 9:00 A.M. to 12 Noon to allow employees to cash their checks.
- D. Because of payroll staff availability, the payroll office is open on Fridays. It is open from 9:00 A.M. to 12 Noon so that distributed paychecks can be cashed at the bank while employees are on their lunch hour.

13.____

Questions 14-16.

DIRECTIONS: In each of Questions 14 through 16, the four sentences are from a paragraph in a report. They are not in the right order. Which of the following arrangements is the BEST one?

14. I. An executive may answer a letter by writing his reply on the face of the letter itself instead of having a return letter typed.
    II. This procedure is efficient because it saves the executive's time, the typist's time, and saves office file space.
    III. Copying machines are used in small offices as well as large offices to save time and money in making brief replies to business letters.
    IV. A copy is made on a copying machine to go into the company files, while the original is mailed back to the sender.
    The CORRECT answer is:

    A. I, II, IV, III
    B. I, IV, II, III
    C. III, I, IV, II
    D. III, IV, II, I

15. I. Most organizations favor one of the types but always include the others to a lesser degree.
    II. However, we can detect a definite trend toward greater use of symbolic control.
    III. We suggest that our local police agencies are today primarily utilizing material control.
    IV. Control can be classified into three types: physical, material, and symbolic.
    The CORRECT answer is:

    A. IV, II, III, I
    B. II, I, IV, III
    C. III, IV, II, I
    D. IV, I, III, II

16. I. They can and do take advantage of ancient political and geographical boundaries, which often give them sanctuary from effective police activity.
    II. This country is essentially a country of small police forces, each operating independently within the limits of its jurisdiction.
    III. The boundaries that define and limit police operations do not hinder the movement of criminals, of course.
    IV. The machinery of law enforcement in America is fragmented, complicated, and frequently overlapping.
    The CORRECT answer is:

    A. III, I, II, IV
    B. II, IV, I, III
    C. IV, II, III, I
    D. IV, III, II, I

17. Examine the following sentence, and then choose from below the words which should be inserted in the blank spaces to produce the best sentence.
    The unit has exceeded _____ goals and the employees are satisfied with _____ accomplishments.

    A. their, it's
    B. it's, it's
    C. its, there
    D. its, their

18. Examine the following sentence, and then choose from below the words which should be inserted in the blank spaces to produce the best sentence.
Research indicates that employees who _____ no opportunity for close social relationships often find their work unsatisfying, and this _____ of satisfaction often reflects itself in low production.

   A. have, lack
   B. have, excess
   C. has, lack
   D. has, excess

19. Words in a sentence must be arranged properly to make sure that the intended meaning of the sentence is clear. The sentence below that does NOT make sense because a clause has been separated from the word on which its meaning depends is:

   A. To be a good writer, clarity is necessary.
   B. To be a good writer, you must write clearly.
   C. You must write clearly to be a good writer.
   D. Clarity is necessary to good writing.

Questions 20-21.

DIRECTIONS: Each of Questions 20 and 21 consists of a statement which contains a word (one of those underlined) that is either incorrectly used because it is not in keeping with the meaning the quotation is evidently intended to convey, or is misspelled. There is only one INCORRECT word in each quotation. Of the four underlined words, determine if the first one should be replaced by the word lettered A, the second one replaced by the word lettered B, the third one replaced by the word lettered C, or the fourth one replaced by the word lettered D. *PRINT THE LETTER OF THE REPLACEMENT WORD YOU HAVE SELECTED IN THE SPACE AT THE RIGHT.*

20. The alleged killer was occasionally permitted to excercise in the corridor.

   A. alledged
   B. ocasionally
   C. permited
   D. exercise

21. Defense counsel stated, in affect, that their conduct was permissible under the First Amendment.

   A. council
   B. effect
   C. there
   D. permissable

Question 22.

DIRECTIONS: Question 22 consists of one sentence. This sentence contains an incorrectly used word. First, decide which is the incorrectly used word. Then, from among the options given, decide which word, when substituted for the incorrectly used word, makes the meaning of the sentence clear.

22. As today's violence has no single cause, so its causes have no single scheme.

   A. deference   B. cure   C. flaw   D. relevance

23. In the sentence, *A man in a light-grey suit waited thirty-five minutes in the ante-room for the all-important document,* the word IMPROPERLY hyphenated is

 A. light-grey
 B. thirty-five
 C. ante-room
 D. all-important

24. In the sentence, *The candidate wants to file his application for preference before it is too late,* the word *before* is used as a(n)

 A. preposition
 B. subordinating conjunction
 C. pronoun
 D. adverb

25. In the sentence, *The perpetrators ran from the scene,* the word *from* is a

 A. preposition
 B. pronoun
 C. verb
 D. conjunction

KEY (CORRECT ANSWERS)

1.	D		11.	D
2.	D		12.	D
3.	A		13.	D
4.	B		14.	C
5.	D		15.	D
6.	D		16.	C
7.	B		17.	D
8.	A		18.	A
9.	C		19.	A
10.	C		20.	D

21. B
22. B
23. C
24. B
25. A

PREPARING WRITTEN MATERIAL

PARAGRAPH REARRANGEMENT
COMMENTARY

The sentences which follow are in scrambled order. You are to rearrange them in proper order and indicate the letter choice containing the correct answer at the space at the right.

Each group of sentences in this section is actually a paragraph presented in scrambled order. Each sentence in the group has a place in that paragraph; no sentence is to be left out. You are to read each group of sentences and decide upon the best order in which to put the sentences so as to form as well-organized paragraph.

The questions in this section measure the ability to solve a problem when all the facts relevant to its solution are not given.

More specifically, certain positions of responsibility and authority require the employee to discover connections between events sometimes, apparently, unrelated. In order to do this, the employee will find it necessary to correctly infer that unspecified events have probably occurred or are likely to occur. This ability becomes especially important when action must be taken on incomplete information.

Accordingly, these questions require competitors to choose among several suggested alternatives, each of which presents a different sequential arrangement of the events. Competitors must choose the MOST logical of the suggested sequences.

In order to do so, they may be required to draw on general knowledge to infer missing concepts or events that are essential to sequencing the given events. Competitors should be careful to infer only what is essential to the sequence. The plausibility of the wrong alternatives will always require the inclusion of unlikely events or of additional chains of events which are NOT essential to sequencing the given events.

It's very important to remember that you are looking for the best of the four possible choices, and that the best choice of all may not even be one of the answers you're given to choose from.

There is no one right way to these problems. Many people have found it helpful to first write out the order of the sentences, as they would have arranged them, on their scrap paper before looking at the possible answers. If their optimum answer is there, this can save them some time. If it isn't, this method can still give insight into solving the problem. Others find it most helpful to just go through each of the possible choices, contrasting each as they go along. You should use whatever method feels comfortable, and works, for you.

While most of these types of questions are not that difficult, we've added a higher percentage of the difficult type, just to give you more practice. Usually there are only one or two questions on this section that contain such subtle distinctions that you're unable to answer confidently, and you then may find yourself stuck deciding between two possible choices, neither of which you're sure about.

EXAMINATION SECTION
TEST 1

DIRECTIONS: The sentences that follow are in scrambled order. You are to rearrange them in proper order and indicate the letter choice containing the correct answer. *PRINT THE LETTER OF THE CORRECT ANSWER IN THE SPACE AT THE RIGHT.*

1. Below are four statements labeled W., X., Y., and Z. 1._____
   W. He was a strict and fanatic drillmaster.
   X. The word is always used in a derogatory sense and generally shows resentment and anger on the part of the user.
   Y. It is from the name of this Frenchman that we derive our English word, martinet.
   Z. Jean Martinet was the Inspector-General of Infantry during the reign of King Louis XIV.

   The *PROPER* order in which these sentences should be placed in a paragraph is:

   A. X, Z, W, Y   B. X, Z, Y, W   C. Z, W, Y, X   D. Z, Y, W, X

2. In the following paragraph, the sentences which are numbered, have been jumbled. 2._____
   1. Since then it has undergone changes.
   2. It was incorporated in 1955 under the laws of the State of New York.
   3. Its primary purpose, a cleaner city, has, however, remained the same.
   4. The Citizens Committee works in cooperation with the Mayor's Inter-departmental Committee for a Clean City.

   The order in which these sentences should be arranged to form a well-organized paragraph is:

   A. 2, 4, 1, 3   B. 3, 4, 1, 2   C. 4, 2, 1, 3   D. 4, 3, 2, 1

Questions 3-5.

DIRECTIONS: The sentences listed below are part of a meaningful paragraph but they are not given in their proper order. You are to decide what would be the *best order* in which to put the sentences so as to form a well-organized paragraph. Each sentence has a place in the paragraph; there are no extra sentences. You are then to answer questions 3 to 5 inclusive on the basis of your rearrangements of these secrambled sentences into a properly organized paragraph.

In 1887 some insurance companies organized an Inspection Department to advise their clients on all phases of fire prevention and protection. Probably this has been due to the smaller annual fire losses in Great Britain than in the United States. It tests various fire prevention devices and appliances and determines manufacturing hazards and their safeguards. Fire research began earlier in the United States and is more advanced than in Great Britain. Later they established a laboratory specializing in electrical, mechanical, hydraulic, and chemical fields.

3. When the five sentences are arranged in proper order, the paragraph starts with the sentence which begins

   A. "In 1887 ..." B. "Probably this ..." C. "It tests ..."
   D. "Fire research ..." E. "Later they ..."

4. In the last sentence listed above, "they" refers to

   A. insurance companies
   B. the United States and Great Britain
   C. the Inspection Department
   D. clients
   E. technicians

5. When the above paragraph is properly arranged, it ends with the words

   A. "... and protection." B. "... the United States."
   C. "... their safeguards." D. "... in Great Britain."
   E. "... chemical fields."

KEY (CORRECT ANSWERS)

1. C
2. C
3. D
4. A
5. C

TEST 2

DIRECTIONS: In each of the questions numbered 1 through 5, several sentences are given. For each question, choose as your answer the group of numbers that represents the *most logical* order of these sentences if they were arranged in paragraph form. *PRINT THE LETTER OF THE CORRECT ANSWER IN THE SPACE AT THE RIGHT.*

1. 1. It is established when one shows that the landlord has prevented the tenant's enjoyment of his interest in the property leased.
    2. Constructive eviction is the result of a breach of the covenant of quiet enjoyment implied in all leases.
    3. In some parts of the United States, it is not complete until the tenant vacates within a reasonable time.
    4. Generally, the acts must be of such serious and permanent character as to deny the tenant the enjoyment of his possessing rights.
    5. In this event, upon abandonment of the premises, the tenant's liability for that ceases.

    The CORRECT answer is:

    A. 2, 1, 4, 3, 5   B. 5, 2, 3, 1, 4   C. 4, 3, 1, 2, 5
    D. 1, 3, 5, 4, 2

    1._____

2. 1. The powerlessness before private and public authorities that is the typical experience of the slum tenant is reminiscent of the situation of blue-collar workers all through the nineteenth century.
    2. Similarly, in recent years, this chapter of history has been reopened by anti-poverty groups which have attempted to organize slum tenants to enable them to bargain collectively with their landlords about the conditions of their tenancies.
    3. It is familiar history that many of the workers remedied their condition by joining together and presenting their demands collectively.
    4. Like the workers, tenants are forced by the conditions of modern life into substantial dependence on these who possess great political arid economic power.
    5. What's more, the very fact of dependence coupled with an absence of education and self-confidence makes them hesitant and unable to stand up for what they need from those in power.

    The CORRECT answer is:

    A. 5, 4, 1, 2, 3   B. 2, 3, 1, 5, 4   C. 3, 1, 5, 4, 2
    D. 1, 4, 5, 3, 2

    2._____

3. 1. A railroad, for example, when not acting as a common carrier may contract; away responsibility for its own negligence.
    2. As to a landlord, however, no decision has been found relating to the legal effect of a clause shifting the statutory duty of repair to the tenant.
    3. The courts have not passed on the validity of clauses relieving the landlord of this duty and liability.
    4. They have, however, upheld the validity of exculpatory clauses in other types of contracts.
    5. Housing regulations impose a duty upon the landlord to maintain leased premises in safe condition.

    3._____

6. As another example, a bailee may limit his liability except for gross negligence, willful acts, or fraud.

The CORRECT answer is:

A. 2, 1, 6, 4, 3, 5   B. 1, 3, 4, 5, 6, 2   C. 3, 5, 1, 4, 2, 6
D. 5, 3, 4, 1, 6, 2

4. 1. Since there are only samples in the building, retail or consumer sales are generally eschewed by mart occupants, and,in some instances, rigid controls are maintained to limit entrance to the mart only to those persons engaged in retailing.
    2. Since World War I, in many larger cities, there has developed a new type of property, called the mart building.
    3. It can, therefore, be used by wholesalers and jobbers for the display of sample merchandise.
    4. This type of building is most frequently a multi-storied, finished interior property which is a cross between a retail arcade and a loft building.
    5. This limitation enables the mart occupants to ship the orders from another location after the retailer or dealer makes his selection from the samples.

The CORRECT answer is:

A. 2, 4, 3, 1, 5   B. 4, 3, 5, 1, 2   C. 1, 3, 2, 4, 5
D. 1, 4, 2, 3, 5

5. 1. In general, staff-line friction reduces the distinctive contribution of staff personnel.
    2. The conflicts, however, introduce an uncontrolled element into the managerial system.
    3. On the other hand, the natural resistance of the line to staff innovations probably usefully restrains over-eager efforts to apply untested procedures on a large scale.
    4. Under such conditions, it is difficult to know when valuable ideas are being sacrificed.
    5. The relatively weak position of staff, requiring accommodation to the line, tends to restrict their ability to engage .in free, experimental innovation.

The CORRECT answer is:

A. 4, 2, 3, 1, 3   B. 1, 5, 3, 2, 4   C. 5, 3, 1, 2, 4
D. 2, 1, 4, 5, 3

KEY (CORRECT ANSWERS)

1. A
2. D
3. D
4. A
5. B

TEST 3

DIRECTIONS: Questions 1 through 4 consist of six sentences which can be arranged in a logical sequence. For each question, select the choice which places the numbered sentences in the *most logical* sequence. PRINT THE LETTER OF THE CORRECT ANSWER IN THE SPACE AT THE RIGHT.

1.
   1. The burden of proof as to each issue is determined before trial and remains upon the same party throughout the trial.
   2. The jury is at liberty to believe one witness' testimony as against a number of contradictory witnesses.
   3. In a civil case, the party bearing the burden of proof is required to prove his contention by a fair preponderance of the evidence.
   4. However, it must be noted that a fair preponderance of evidence does not necessarily mean a greater number of witnesses.
   5. The burden of proof is the burden which rests upon one of the parties to an action to persuade the trier of the facts, generally the jury, that a proposition he asserts is true.
   6. If the evidence is equally balanced, or if it leaves the jury in such doubt as to be unable to decide the controversy either way, judgment must be given against the party upon whom the burden of proof rests.

   The CORRECT answer is:

   A. 3, 2, 5, 4, 1, 6   B. 1, 2, 6, 5, 3, 4   C. 3, 4, 5, 1, 2, 6
   D. 5, 1, 3, 6, 4, 2

   1.____

2.
   1. If a parent is without assets and is unemployed, he cannot be convicted of the crime of non-support of a child.
   2. The term "sufficient ability" has been held to mean sufficient financial ability.
   3. It does not matter if his unemployment is by choice or unavoidable circumstances.
   4. If he fails to take any steps at all, he may be liable to prosecution for endangering the welfare of a child.
   5. Under the penal law, a parent is responsible for the support of his minor child only if the parent is "of sufficient ability."
   6. An indigent parent may meet his obligation by borrowing money or by seeking aid under the provisions of the Social Welfare Law.

   The CORRECT answer is:

   A. 6, 1, 5, 3, 2, 4   B. 1, 3, 5, 2, 4, 6   C. 5, 2, 1, 3, 6, 4
   D. 1, 6, 4, 5, 2, 3

   2.____

3.
1. Consider, for example, the case of a rabble rouser who urges a group of twenty people to go out and break the windows of a nearby factory.
2. Therefore, the law fills the indicated gap with the crime of inciting to riot."
3. A person is considered guilty of inciting to riot when he urges ten or more persons to engage in tumultuous and violent conduct of a kind likely to create public alarm.
4. However, if he has not obtained the cooperation of at least four people, he cannot be charged with unlawful assembly.
5. The charge of inciting to riot was added to the law to cover types of conduct which cannot be classified as either the crime of "riot" or the crime of "unlawful assembly."
6. If he acquires the acquiescence of at least four of them, he is guilty of unlawful assembly even if the project does not materialize.

The CORRECT answer is:

A. 3, 5, 1, 6, 4, 2 B. 5, 1, 4, 6, 2, 3 C. 3, 4, 1, 5, 2, 6
D. 5, 1, 4, 6, 3, 2

4.
1. If, however, the rebuttal evidence presents an issue of credibility, it is for the jury to determine whether the presumption has, in fact, been destroyed.
2. Once sufficient evidence to the contrary is introduced, the presumption disappears from the trial.
3. The effect of a presumption is to place the burden upon the adversary to come forward with evidence to rebut the presumption.
4. When a presumption is overcome and ceases to exist in the case, the fact or facts which gave rise to the presumption still remain.
5. Whether a presumption has been overcome is ordinarily a question for the court.
6. Such information may furnish a basis for a logical inference.

The CORRECT answer is:

A. 4, 6, 2, 5, 1, 3 B. 3, 2, 5, 1, 4, 6 C. 5, 3, 6, 4, 2, 1
D. 5, 4, 1, 2, 6, 3

KEY (CORRECT ANSWERS)

1. D
2. C
3. A
4. B

PHILOSOPHY, PRINCIPLES, PRACTICES AND TECHNICS
OF
SUPERVISION, ADMINISTRATION, MANAGEMENT AND ORGANIZATION

TABLE OF CONTENTS

		Page
I.	MEANING OF SUPERVISION	1
II.	THE OLD AND THE NEW SUPERVISION	1
III.	THE EIGHT (8) BASIC PRINCIPLES OF THE NEW SUPERVISION	1
	1. Principle of Responsibility	1
	2. Principle of Authority	2
	3. Principle of Self-Growth	2
	4. Principle of Individual Worth	2
	5. Principle of Creative Leadership	2
	6. Principle of Success and Failure	2
	7. Principle of Science	3
	8. Principle of Cooperation	3
IV.	WHAT IS ADMINISTRATION?	3
	1. Practices commonly classed as "Supervisory"	3
	2. Practices commonly classed as "Administrative"	3
	3. Practices classified as both "Supervisory" and "Administrative"	4
V.	RESPONSIBILITIES OF THE SUPERVISOR	4
VI.	COMPETENCIES OF THE SUPERVISOR	4
VII.	THE PROFESSIONAL SUPERVISOR—EMPLOYEE RELATIONSHIP	4
VIII.	MINI-TEXT IN SUPERVISION, ADMINISTRATION, MANAGEMENT AND ORGANIZATION	5
	A. Brief Highlights	5
	1. Levels of Management	5
	2. What the Supervisor Must Learn	6
	3. A Definition of Supervision	6
	4. Elements of the Team Concept	6
	5. Principles of Organization	6
	6. The Four Important Parts of Every Job	6
	7. Principles of Delegation	6
	8. Principles of Effective Communications	7
	9. Principles of Work Improvement	7

TABLE OF CONTENTS (CONTINUED)

10. Areas of Job Improvement	7
11. Seven Key Points in Making Improvements	7
12. Corrective Techniques for Job Improvement	7
13. A Planning Checklist	8
14. Five Characteristics of Good Directions	8
15. Types of Directions	8
16. Controls	8
17. Orienting the New Employee	8
18. Checklist for Orienting New Employees	8
19. Principles of Learning	9
20. Causes of Poor Performance	9
21. Four Major Steps in On-The-Job Instructions	9
22. Employees Want Five Things	9
23. Some Don'ts in Regard to Praise	9
24. How to Gain Your Workers' Confidence	9
25. Sources of Employee Problems	9
26. The Supervisor's Key to Discipline	10
27. Five Important Processes of Management	10
28. When the Supervisor Fails to Plan	10
29. Fourteen General Principles of Management	10
30. Change	10

B. Brief Topical Summaries 11
    I.   Who/What is the Supervisor? 11
    II.   The Sociology of Work 11
    III.   Principles and Practices of Supervision 12
    IV.   Dynamic Leadership 12
    V.   Processes for Solving Problems 12
    VI.   Training for Results 13
    VII.   Health, Safety and Accident Prevention 13
    VIII.   Equal Employment Opportunity 13
    IX.   Improving Communications 14
    X.   Self-Development 14
    XI.   Teaching and Training 14
        A. The Teaching Process 14
            1. Preparation 14
            2. Presentation 15
            3. Summary 15
            4. Application 15
            5. Evaluation 15
        B. Teaching Methods 15
            1. Lecture 15
            2. Discussion 15
            3. Demonstration 16
            4. Performance 16
            5. Which Method to Use 16

PHILOSOPHY, PRINCIPLES, PRACTICES, AND TECHNICS
OF
SUPERVISION, ADMINISTRATION, MANAGEMENT AND ORGANIZATION

I. MEANING OF SUPERVISION

The extension of the democratic philosophy has been accompanied by an extension in the scope of supervision. Modern leaders and supervisors no longer think of supervision in the narrow sense of being confined chiefly to visiting employees, supplying materials, or rating the staff. They regard supervision as being intimately related to all the concerned agencies of society, they speak of the supervisor's function in terms of "growth", rather than the "improvement," of employees.

This modern concept of supervision may be defined as follows:

Supervision is leadership and the development of leadership within groups which are cooperatively engaged in inspection, research, training, guidance and evaluation.

II. THE OLD AND THE NEW SUPERVISION

TRADITIONAL
1. Inspection
2. Focused on the employee
3. Visitation
4. Random and haphazard
5. Imposed and authoritarian
6. One person usually

MODERN
1. Study and analysis
2. Focused on aims, materials, methods, supervisors, employees, environment
3. Demonstrations, intervisitation, workshops, directed reading, bulletins, etc.
4. Definitely organized and planned (scientific)
5. Cooperative and democratic
6. Many persons involved (creative)

III THE EIGHT (8) BASIC PRINCIPLES OF THE NEW SUPERVISION

1. *PRINCIPLE OF RESPONSIBILITY*
Authority to act and responsibility for acting must be joined.
    a. If you give responsibility, give authority.
    b. Define employee duties clearly.
    c. Protect employees from criticism by others.
    d. Recognize the rights as well as obligations of employees.
    e. Achieve the aims of a democratic society insofar as it is possible within the area of your work.
    f. Establish a situation favorable to training and learning.
    g. Accept ultimate responsibility for everything done in your section, unit, office, division, department.
    h. Good administration and good supervision are inseparable.

2. PRINCIPLE OF AUTHORITY

The success of the supervisor is measured by the extent to which the power of authority is not used.

    a. Exercise simplicity and informality in supervision.
    b. Use the simplest machinery of supervision.
    c. If it is good for the organization as a whole, it is probably justified.
    d. Seldom be arbitrary or authoritative.
    e. Do not base your work on the power of position or of personality.
    f. Permit and encourage the free expression of opinions.

3. PRINCIPLE OF SELF-GROWTH

The success of the supervisor is measured by the extent to which, and the speed with which, he is no longer needed.

    a. Base criticism on principles, not on specifics.
    b. Point out higher activities to employees.
    c. Train for self-thinking by employees, to meet new situations.
    d. Stimulate initiative, self-reliance and individual responsibility.
    e. Concentrate on stimulating the growth of employees rather than on removing defects.

4. PRINCIPLE OF INDIVIDUAL WORTH

Respect for the individual is a paramount consideration in supervision.

    a. Be human and sympathetic in dealing with employees.
    b. Don't nag about things to be done.
    c. Recognize the individual differences among employees and seek opportunities to permit best expression of each personality.

5. PRINCIPLE OF CREATIVE LEADERSHIP

The best supervision is that which is not apparent to the employee.

    a. Stimulate, don't drive employees to creative action.
    b. Emphasize doing good things.
    c. Encourage employees to do what they do best.
    d. Do not be too greatly concerned with details of subject or method.
    e. Do not be concerned exclusively with immediate problems and activities.
    f. Reveal higher activities and make them both desired and maximally possible.
    g. Determine procedures in the light of each situation but see that these are derived from a sound basic philosophy.
    h. Aid, inspire and lead so as to liberate the creative spirit latent in all good employees.

6. PRINCIPLE OF SUCCESS AND FAILURE

There are no unsuccessful employees, only unsuccessful supervisors who have failed to give proper leadership.

    a. Adapt suggestions to the capacities, attitudes, and prejudices of employees.
    b. Be gradual, be progressive, be persistent.
    c. Help the employee find the general principle; have the employee apply his own problem to the general principle.
    d. Give adequate appreciation for good work and honest effort.
    e. Anticipate employee difficulties and help to prevent them.
    f. Encourage employees to do the desirable things they will do anyway.
    g. Judge your supervision by the results it secures.

7. PRINCIPLE OF SCIENCE

Successful supervision is scientific, objective, and experimental. It is based on facts, not on prejudices.

      a. Be cumulative in results.
      b. Never divorce your suggestions from the goals of training.
      c. Don't be impatient of results.
      d. Keep all matters on a professional, not a personal level.
      e. Do not be concerned exclusively with immediate problems and activities.
      f. Use objective means of determining achievement and rating where possible.

8. PRINCIPLE OF COOPERATION

Supervision is a cooperative enterprise between supervisor and employee.

      a. Begin with conditions as they are.
      b. Ask opinions of all involved when formulating policies.
      c. Organization is as good as its weakest link.
      d. Let employees help to determine policies and department programs.
      e. Be approachable and accessible - physically and mentally.
      f. Develop pleasant social relationships.

IV. WHAT IS ADMINISTRATION?

Administration is concerned with providing the environment, the material facilities, and the operational procedures that will promote the maximum growth and development of supervisors and employees. (Organization is an aspect, and a concomitant, of administration.)

There is no sharp line of demarcation between supervision and administration; these functions are intimately interrelated and, often, overlapping. They are complementary activities.

1. PRACTICES COMMONLY CLASSED AS "SUPERVISORY"
      a. Conducting employees conferences
      b. Visiting sections, units, offices, divisions, departments
      c. Arranging for demonstrations
      d. Examining plans
      e. Suggesting professional reading
      f. Interpreting bulletins
      g. Recommending in-service training courses
      h. Encouraging experimentation
      i. Appraising employee morale
      j. Providing for intervisitation

2. PRACTICES COMMONLY CLASSIFIED AS "ADMINISTRATIVE"
      a. Management of the office
      b. Arrangement of schedules for extra duties
      c. Assignment of rooms or areas
      d. Distribution of supplies
      e. Keeping records and reports
      f. Care of audio-visual materials
      g. Keeping inventory records
      h. Checking record cards and books
      i. Programming special activities
      j. Checking on the attendance and punctuality of employees

3. *PRACTICES COMMONLY CLASSIFIED AS BOTH "SUPERVISORY" AND "ADMINISTRATIVE"*
   a. Program construction
   b. Testing or evaluating outcomes
   c. Personnel accounting
   d. Ordering instructional materials

V. RESPONSIBILITIES OF THE SUPERVISOR

A person employed in a supervisory capacity must constantly be able to improve his own efficiency and ability. He represents the employer to the employees and only continuous self-examination can make him a capable supervisor.

Leadership and training are the supervisor's responsibility. An efficient working unit is one in which the employees work with the supervisor. It is his job to bring out the best in his employees. He must always be relaxed, courteous and calm in his association with his employees. Their feelings are important, and a harsh attitude does not develop the most efficient employees.

VI. COMPETENCIES OF THE SUPERVISOR

1. Complete knowledge of the duties and responsibilities of his position.
2. To be able to organize a job, plan ahead and carry through.
3. To have self-confidence and initiative.
4. To be able to handle the unexpected situation and make quick decisions.
5. To be able to properly train subordinates in the positions they are best suited for.
6. To be able to keep good human relations among his subordinates.
7. To be able to keep good human relations between his subordinates and himself and to earn their respect and trust.

VII. THE PROFESSIONAL SUPERVISOR-EMPLOYEE RELATIONSHIP

There are two kinds of efficiency: one kind is only apparent and is produced in organizations through the exercise of mere discipline; this is but a simulation of the second, or true, efficiency which springs from spontaneous cooperation. If you are a manager, no matter how great or small your responsibility, it is your job, in the final analysis, to create and develop this involuntary cooperation among the people whom you supervise. For, no matter how powerful a combination of money, machines, and materials a company may have, this is a dead and sterile thing without a team of willing, thinking and articulate people to guide it.

The following 21 points are presented as indicative of the exemplary basic relationship that should exist between supervisor and employee:

1. Each person wants to be liked and respected by his fellow employee and wants to be treated with consideration and respect by his superior.
2. The most competent employee will make an error. However, in a unit where good relations exist between the supervisor and his employees, tenseness and fear do not exist. Thus, errors are not hidden or covered up and the efficiency of a unit is not impaired.
3. Subordinates resent rules, regulations, or orders that are unreasonable or unexplained.
4. Subordinates are quick to resent unfairness, harshness, injustices and favoritism.
5. An employee will accept responsibility if he knows that he will be complimented for a job well done, and not too harshly chastised for failure; that his supervisor will check the cause of the failure, and, if it was the supervisor's fault, he will assume the blame therefore. If it was the employee's fault, his supervisor will explain the correct method or means of handling the responsibility.

6. An employee wants to receive credit for a suggestion he has made, that is used. If a suggestion cannot be used, the employee is entitled to an explanation. The supervisor should not say "no" and close the subject.
7. Fear and worry slow up a worker's ability. Poor working environment can impair his physical and mental health. A good supervisor avoids forceful methods, threats and arguments to get a job done.
8. A forceful supervisor is able to train his employees individually and as a team, and is able to motivate them in the proper channels.
9. A mature supervisor is able to properly evaluate his subordinates and to keep them happy and satisfied.
10. A sensitive supervisor will never patronize his subordinates.
11. A worthy supervisor will respect his employees' confidences.
12. Definite and clear-cut responsibilities should be assigned to each executive.
13. Responsibility should always be coupled with corresponding authority.
14. No change should be made in the scope or responsibilities of a position without a definite understanding to that effect on the part of all persons concerned.
15. No executive or employee, occupying a single position in the organization, should be subject to definite orders from more than one source.
16. Orders should never be given to subordinates over the head of a responsible executive. Rather than do this, the officer in question should be supplanted.
17. Criticisms of subordinates should, whoever possible, be made privately, and in no case should a subordinate be criticized in the presence of executives or employees of equal or lower rank.
18. No dispute or difference between executives or employees as to authority or responsibilities should be considered too trivial for prompt and careful adjudication.
19. Promotions, wage changes, and disciplinary action should always be approved by the executive immediately superior to the one directly responsible.
20. No executive or employee should ever be required, or expected, to be at the same time an assistant to, and critic of, another.
21. Any executive whose work is subject to regular inspection should, whever practicable, be given the assistance and facilities necessary to enable him to maintain an independent check of the quality of his work.

VIII. MINI-TEXT IN SUPERVISION, ADMINISTRATION, MANAGEMENT, AND ORGANIZATION

A. BRIEF HIGHLIGHTS

Listed concisely and sequentially are major headings and important data in the field for quick recall and review.

1. *LEVELS OF MANAGEMENT*

   Any organization of some size has several levels of management. In terms of a ladder the levels are:

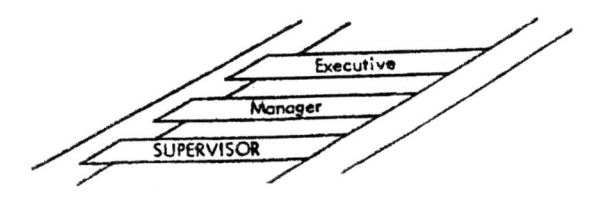

   - Executive
   - Manager
   - SUPERVISOR

The first level is very important because it is the beginning point of management leadership.

2. WHAT THE SUPERVISOR MUST LEARN
A supervisor must learn to:
(1) Deal with people and their differences
(2) Get the job done through people
(3) Recognize the problems when they exist
(4) Overcome obstacles to good performance
(5) Evaluate the performance of people
(6) Check his own performance in terms of accomplishment

3. A DEFINITION OF SUPERVISOR
The term supervisor means any individual having authority, in the interests of the employer, to hire, transfer, suspend, lay-off, recall, promote, discharge, assign, reward, or discipline other employees or responsibility to direct them, or to adjust their grievances, or effectively to recommend such action, if, in connection with the foregoing, exercise of such authority is not of a merely routine or clerical nature but requires the use of independent judgment.

4. ELEMENTS OF THE TEAM CONCEPT
What is involved in teamwork? The component parts are:
(1) Members   (3) Goals   (5) Cooperation
(2) A leader   (4) Plans   (6) Spirit

5. PRINCIPLES OF ORGANIZATION
(1) A team member must know what his job is.
(2) Be sure that the nature and scope of a job are understood.
(3) Authority and responsibility should be carefully spelled out.
(4) A supervisor should be permitted to make the maximum number of decisions affecting his employees.
(5) Employees should report to only one supervisor.
(6) A supervisor should direct only as many employees as he can handle effectively.
(7) An organization plan should be flexible.
(8) Inspection and performance of work should be separate.
(9) Organizational problems should receive immediate attention.
(10) Assign work in line with ability and experience.

6. THE FOUR IMPORTANT PARTS OF EVERY JOB
(1) Inherent in every job is the *accountability* for results.
(2) A second set of factors in every job is *responsibilities*.
(3) Along with duties and responsibilities one must have the *authority* to act within certain limits without obtaining permission to proceed.
(4) No job exists in a vacuum. The supervisor is surrounded by key *relationships*.

7. PRINCIPLES OF DELEGATION
Where work is delegated for the first time, the supervisor should think in terms of these questions:
(1) Who is best qualified to do this?
(2) Can an employee improve his abilities by doing this?
(3) How long should an employee spend on this?
(4) Are there any special problems for which he will need guidance?
(5) How broad a delegation can I make?

8. PRINCIPLES OF EFFECTIVE COMMUNICATIONS
    (1) Determine the media
    (2) To whom directed?
    (3) Identification and source authority
    (4) Is communication understood?

9. PRINCIPLES OF WORK IMPROVEMENT
    (1) Most people usually do only the work which is assigned to them
    (2) Workers are likely to fit assigned work into the time available to perform it
    (3) A good workload usually stimulates output
    (4) People usually do their best work when they know that results will be reviewed or inspected
    (5) Employees usually feel that someone else is responsible for conditions of work, workplace layout, job methods, type of tools/equipment, and other such factors
    (6) Employees are usually defensive about their job security
    (7) Employees have natural resistance to change
    (8) Employees can support or destroy a supervisor
    (9) A supervisor usually earns the respect of his people through his personal example of diligence and efficiency

10. AREAS OF JOB IMPROVEMENT
The areas of job improvement are quite numerous, but the most common ones which a supervisor can identify and utilize are:

    (1) Departmental layout   (5) Work methods
    (2) Flow of work   (6) Materials handling
    (3) Workplace layout   (7) Utilization
    (4) Utilization of manpower   (8) Motion economy

11. SEVEN KEY POINTS IN MAKING IMPROVEMENTS
    (1) Select the job to be improved
    (2) Study how it is being done now
    (3) Question the present method
    (4) Determine actions to be taken
    (5) Chart proposed method
    (6) Get approval and apply
    (7) Solicit worker participation

12. CORRECTIVE TECHNIQUES OF JOB IMPROVEMENT

Specific Problems	General Improvement	Corrective Techniques
(1) Size of workload	(1) Departmental layout	(1) Study with scale model
(2) Inability to meet schedules	(2) Flow of work	(2) Flow chart study
(3) Strain and fatigue	(3) Work plan layout	(3) Motion analysis
(4) Improper use of men and skills	(4) Utilization of manpower	(4) Comparison of units produced to standard allowance
(5) Waste, poor quality, unsafe conditions	(5) Work methods	(5) Methods analysis
(6) Bottleneck conditions that hinder output	(6) Materials handling	(6) Flow chart & equipment study
(7) Poor utilization of equipment and machine	(7) Utilization of equipment	(7) Down time vs. running time
(8) Efficiency and productivity of labor	(8) Motion economy	(8) Motion analysis

13. A *PLANNING CHECKLIST*

(1) Objectives	(6) Resources	(11) Safety
(2) Controls	(7) Manpower	(12) Money
(3) Delegations	(8) Equipment	(13) Work
(4) Communications	(9) Supplies and materials	(14) Timing of improvements
(5) Resources	(10) Utilization of time	

14. *FIVE CHARACTERISTICS OF GOOD DIRECTIONS*

In order to get results, directions must be:
(1) Possible of accomplishment   (3) Related to mission   (5) Unmistakably clear
(2) Agreeable with worker interests   (4) Planned and complete

15. *TYPES OF DIRECTIONS*
(1) Demands or direct orders   (3) Suggestion or implication
(2) Requests   (4) Volunteering

16. *CONTROLS*

A typical listing of the overall areas in which the supervisor should establish controls might be:

(1) Manpower	(3) Quality of work	(5) Time	(7) Money
(2) Materials	(4) Quantity of work	(6) Space	(8) Methods

17. *ORIENTING THE NEW EMPLOYEE*
(1) Prepare for him   (3) Orientation for the job
(2) Welcome the new employee   (4) Follow-up

18. *CHECKLIST FOR ORIENTING NEW EMPLOYEES*   Yes   No

(1) Do your appreciate the feelings of new employees when they first report for work?
(2) Are you aware of the fact that the new employee must make a big adjustment to his job?
(3) Have you given him good reasons for liking the job and the organization?
(4) Have you prepared for his first day on the job?
(5) Did you welcome him cordially and make him feel needed?
(6) Did you establish rapport with him so that he feels free to talk and discuss matters with you?
(7) Did you explain his job to him and his relationship to you?
(8) Does he know that his work will be evaluated periodically on a basis that is fair and objective?
(9) Did you introduce him to his fellow workers in such a way that they are likely to accept him?
(10) Does he know what employee benefits he will receive?
(11) Does he understand the importance of being on the job and what to do if he must leave his duty station?
(12) Has he been impressed with the importance of accident prevention and safe practice?
(13) Does he generally know his way around the department?
(14) Is he under the guidance of a sponsor who will teach the right ways of doing things?
(15) Do you plan to follow-up so that he will continue to adjust successfully to his job?

19. *PRINCIPLES OF LEARNING*
> (1) Motivation   (2) Demonstration or explanation   (3) Practice

20. *CAUSES OF POOR PERFORMANCE*
> (1) Improper training for job
> (2) Wrong tools
> (3) Inadequate directions
> (4) Lack of supervisory follow-up
> (5) Poor communications
> (6) Lack of standards of performance
> (7) Wrong work habits
> (8) Low morale
> (9) Other

21. *FOUR MAJOR STEPS IN ON-THE-JOB INSTRUCTION*
> (1) Prepare the worker
> (2) Present the operation
> (3) Tryout performance
> (4) Follow-up

22. *EMPLOYEES WANT FIVE THINGS*
> (1) Security (2) Opportunity (3) Recognition (4) Inclusion (5) Expression

23. *SOME DON'TS IN REGARD TO PRAISE*
> (1) Don't praise a person for something he hasn't done
> (2) Don't praise a person unless you can be sincere
> (3) Don't be sparing in praise just because your superior withholds it from you
> (4) Don't let too much time elapse between good performance and recognition of it

24. *HOW TO GAIN YOUR WORKERS' CONFIDENCE*
Methods of developing confidence include such things as:
> (1) Knowing the interests, habits, hobbies of employees
> (2) Admitting your own inadequacies
> (3) Sharing and telling of confidence in others
> (4) Supporting people when they are in trouble
> (5) Delegating matters that can be well handled
> (6) Being frank and straightforward about problems and working conditions
> (7) Encouraging others to bring their problems to you
> (8) Taking action on problems which impede worker progress

25. *SOURCES OF EMPLOYEE PROBLEMS*
On-the-job causes might be such things as:
> (1) A feeling that favoritism is exercised in assignments
> (2) Assignment of overtime
> (3) An undue amount of supervision
> (4) Changing methods or systems
> (5) Stealing of ideas or trade secrets
> (6) Lack of interest in job
> (7) Threat of reduction in force
> (8) Ignorance or lack of communications
> (9) Poor equipment
> (10) Lack of knowing how supervisor feels toward employee
> (11) Shift assignments

Off-the-job problems might have to do with:
> (1) Health   (2) Finances   (3) Housing   (4) Family

26. THE SUPERVISOR'S KEY TO DISCIPLINE

There are several key points about discipline which the supervisor should keep in mind:
(1) Job discipline is one of the disciplines of life and is directed by the supervisor.
(2) It is more important to correct an employee fault than to fix blame for it.
(3) Employee performance is affected by problems both on the job and off.
(4) Sudden or abrupt changes in behavior can be indications of important employee problems.
(5) Problems should be dealt with as soon as possible after they are identified.
(6) The attitude of the supervisor may have more to do with solving problems than the techniques of problem solving.
(7) Correction of employee behavior should be resorted to only after the supervisor is sure that training or counseling will not be helpful.
(8) Be sure to document your disciplinary actions.
(9) Make sure that you are disciplining on the basis of facts rather than personal feelings.
(10) Take each disciplinary step in order, being careful not to make snap judgments, or decisions based on impatience.

27. FIVE IMPORTANT PROCESSES OF MANAGEMENT

(1) Planning   (2) Organizing   (3) Scheduling
(4) Controlling   (5) Motivating

28. WHEN THE SUPERVISOR FAILS TO PLAN

(1) Supervisor creates impression of not knowing his job
(2) May lead to excessive overtime
(3) Job runs itself -- supervisor lacks control
(4) Deadlines and appointments missed
(5) Parts of the work go undone
(6) Work interrupted by emergencies
(7) Sets a bad example
(8) Uneven workload creates peaks and valleys
(9) Too much time on minor details at expense of more important tasks

29. FOURTEEN GENERAL PRINCIPLES OF MANAGEMENT

(1) Division of work
(2) Authority and responsibility
(3) Discipline
(4) Unity of command
(5) Unity of direction
(6) Subordination of individual interest to general interest
(7) Remuneration of personnel
(8) Centralization
(9) Scalar chain
(10) Order
(11) Equity
(12) Stability of tenure of personnel
(13) Initiative
(14) Esprit de corps

30. CHANGE

Bringing about change is perhaps attempted more often, and yet less well understood, than anything else the supervisor does. How do people generally react to change? (People tend to resist change that is imposed upon them by other individuals or circumstances.

Change is characteristic of every situation. It is a part of every real endeavor where the efforts of people are concerned.

A. Why do people resist change?
  People may resist change because of:
    (1) Fear of the unknown
    (2) Implied criticism
    (3) Unpleasant experiences in the past
    (4) Fear of loss of status
    (5) Threat to the ego
    (6) Fear of loss of economic stability

B. How can we best overcome the resistance to change?
  In initiating change, take these steps:
    (1) Get ready to sell
    (2) Identify sources of help
    (3) Anticipate objections
    (4) Sell benefits
    (5) Listen in depth
    (6) Follow up

B. BRIEF TOPICAL SUMMARIES

I. WHO/WHAT IS THE SUPERVISOR?
1. The supervisor is often called the "highest level employee and the lowest level manager."
2. A supervisor is a member of both management and the work group. He acts as a bridge between the two.
3. Most problems in supervision are in the area of human relations, or people problems.
4. Employees expect: Respect, opportunity to learn and to advance, and a sense of belonging, and so forth.
5. Supervisors are responsible for directing people and organizing work. Planning is of paramount importance.
6. A position description is a set of duties and responsibilities inherent to a given position.
7. It is important to keep the position description up-to-date and to provide each employee with his own copy.

II. THE SOCIOLOGY OF WORK
1. People are alike in many ways; however, each individual is unique.
2. The supervisor is challenged in getting to know employee differences. Acquiring skills in evaluating individuals is an asset.
3. Maintaining meaningful working relationships in the organization is of great importance.
4. The supervisor has an obligation to help individuals to develop to their fullest potential.
5. Job rotation on a planned basis helps to build versatility and to maintain interest and enthusiasm in work groups.
6. Cross training (job rotation) provides backup skills.
7. The supervisor can help reduce tension by maintaining a sense of humor, providing guidance to employees, and by making reasonable and timely decisions. Employees respond favorably to working under reasonably predictable circumstances.
8. Change is characteristic of all managerial behavior. The supervisor must adjust to changes in procedures, new methods, technological changes, and to a number of new and sometimes challenging situations.
9. To overcome the natural tendency for people to resist change, the supervisor should become more skillful in initiating change.

III. PRINCIPLES AND PRACTICES OF SUPERVISION
1. Employees should be required to answer to only one superior.
2. A supervisor can effectively direct only a limited number of employees, depending upon the complexity, variety, and proximity of the jobs involved.
3. The organizational chart presents the organization in graphic form. It reflects lines of authority and responsibility as well as interrelationships of units within the organization.
4. Distribution of work can be improved through an analysis using the "Work Distribution Chart."
5. The "Work Distribution Chart" reflects the division of work within a unit in understandable form.
6. When related tasks are given to an employee, he has a better chance of increasing his skills through training.
7. The individual who is given the responsibility for tasks must also be given the appropriate authority to insure adequate results.
8. The supervisor should delegate repetitive, routine work. Preparation of recurring reports, maintaining leave and attendance records are some examples.
9. Good discipline is essential to good task performance. Discipline is reflected in the actions of employees on the job in the absence of supervision.
10. Disciplinary action may have to be taken when the positive aspects of discipline have failed. Reprimand, warning, and suspension are examples of disciplinary action.
11. If a situation calls for a reprimand, be sure it is deserved and remember it is to be done in private.

IV. DYNAMIC LEADERSHIP
1. A style is a personal method or manner of exerting influence.
2. Authoritarian leaders often see themselves as the source of power and authority.
3. The democratic leader often perceives the group as the source of authority and power.
4. Supervisors tend to do better when using the pattern of leadership that is most natural for them.
5. Social scientists suggest that the effective supervisor use the leadership style that best fits the problem or circumstances involved.
6. All four styles -- telling, selling, consulting, joining -- have their place. Using one does not preclude using the other at another time.
7. The theory X point of view assumes that the average person dislikes work, will avoid it whenever possible, and must be coerced to achieve organizational objectives.
8. The theory Y point of view assumes that the average person considers work to be as natural as play, and, when the individual is committed, he requires little supervision or direction to accomplish desired objectives.
9. The leader's basic assumptions concerning human behavior and human nature affect his actions, decisions, and other managerial practices.
10. Dissatisfaction among employees is often present, but difficult to isolate. The supervisor should seek to weaken dissatisfaction by keeping promises, being sincere and considerate, keeping employees informed, and so forth.
11. Constructive suggestions should be encouraged during the natural progress of the work.

V. PROCESSES FOR SOLVING PROBLEMS
1. People find their daily tasks more meaningful and satisfying when they can improve them.
2. The causes of problems, or the key factors, are often hidden in the background. Ability to solve problems often involves the ability to isolate them from their backgrounds. There is some substance to the cliché that some persons "can't see the forest for the trees."
3. New procedures are often developed from old ones. Problems should be broken down into manageable parts. New ideas can be adapted from old ones.

4. People think differently in problem-solving situations. Using a logical, patterned approach is often useful. One approach found to be useful includes these steps:
    (a) Define the problem   (d) Weigh and decide
    (b) Establish objectives   (e) Take action
    (c) Get the facts   (f) Evaluate action

VI. TRAINING FOR RESULTS
1. Participants respond best when they feel training is important to them.
2. The supervisor has responsibility for the training and development of those who report to him.
3. When training is delegated to others, great care must be exercised to insure the trainer has knowledge, aptitude, and interest for his work as a trainer.
4. Training (learning) of some type goes on continually. The most successful supervisor makes certain the learning contributes in a productive manner to operational goals.
5. New employees are particularly susceptible to training. Older employees facing new job situations require specific training, as well as having need for development and growth opportunities.
6. Training needs require continuous monitoring.
7. The training officer of an agency is a professional with a responsibility to assist supervisors in solving training problems.
8. Many of the self-development steps important to the supervisor's own growth are equally important to the development of peers and subordinates. Knowledge of these is important when the supervisor consults with others on development and growth opportunities.

VII. HEALTH, SAFETY, AND ACCIDENT PREVENTION
1. Management-minded supervisors take appropriate measures to assist employees in maintaining health and in assuring safe practices in the work environment.
2. Effective safety training and practices help to avoid injury and accidents.
3. Safety should be a management goal. All infractions of safety which are observed should be corrected without exception.
4. Employees' safety attitude, training and instruction, provision of safe tools and equipment, supervision, and leadership are considered highly important factors which contribute to safety and which can be influenced directly by supervisors.
5. When accidents do occur they should be investigated promptly for very important reasons, including the fact that information which is gained can be used to prevent accidents in the future.

VIII. EQUAL EMPLOYMENT OPPORTUNITY
1. The supervisor should endeavor to treat all employees fairly, without regard to religion, race, sex, or national origin.
2. Groups tend to reflect the attitude of the leader. Prejudice can be detected even in very subtle form. Supervisors must strive to create a feeling of mutual respect and confidence in every employee.
3. Complete utilization of all human resources is a national goal. Equitable consideration should be accorded women in the work force, minority-group members, the physically and mentally handicapped, and the older employee. The important question is: "Who can do the job?"
4. Training opportunities, recognition for performance, overtime assignments, promotional opportunities, and all other personnel actions are to be handled on an equitable basis.

IX. IMPROVING COMMUNICATIONS

1. Communications is achieving understanding between the sender and the receiver of a message. It also means sharing information -- the creation of understanding.
2. Communication is basic to all human activity. Words are means of conveying meanings; however, real meanings are in people.
3. There are very practical differences in the effectiveness of one-way, impersonal, and two-way communications. Words spoken face-to-face are better understood. Telephone conversations are effective, but lack the rapport of person-to-person exchanges. The whole person communicates.
4. Cooperation and communication in an organization go hand in hand. When there is a mutual respect between people, spelling out rules and procedures for communicating is unnecessary.
5. There are several barriers to effective communications. These include failure to listen with respect and understanding, lack of skill in feedback, and misinterpreting the meanings of words used by the speaker. It is also common practice to listen to what we want to hear, and tune out things we do not want to hear.
6. Communication is management's chief problem. The supervisor should accept the challenge to communicate more effectively and to improve interagency and intra-agency communications.
7. The supervisor may often plan for and conduct meetings. The planning phase is critical and may determine the success or the failure of a meeting.
8. Speaking before groups usually requires extra effort. Stage fright may never disappear completely, but it can be controlled.

X. SELF-DEVELOPMENT

1. Every employee is responsible for his own self-development.
2. Toastmaster and toastmistress clubs offer opportunities to improve skills in oral communications.
3. Planning for one's own self-development is of vital importance. Supervisors know their own strengths and limitations better than anyone else.
4. Many opportunities are open to aid the supervisor in his developmental efforts, including job assignments; training opportunities, both governmental and non-governmental -- to include universities and professional conferences and seminars.
5. Programmed instruction offers a means of studying at one's own rate.
6. Where difficulties may arise from a supervisor's being away from his work for training, he may participate in televised home study or correspondence courses to meet his self-develop- ment needs.

XI. TEACHING AND TRAINING

A. The Teaching Process

Teaching is encouraging and guiding the learning activities of students toward established goals. In most cases this process consists in five steps: preparation, presentation, summarization, evaluation, and application.

1. Preparation

Preparation is twofold in nature; that of the supervisor and the employee.
Preparation by the supervisor is absolutely essential to success. He must know what, when, where, how, and whom he will teach. Some of the factors that should be considered are:

(1) The objectives
(2) The materials needed
(3) The methods to be used
(4) Employee participation
(5) Employee interest
(6) Training aids
(7) Evaluation
(8) Summarization

Employee preparation consists in preparing the employee to receive the material. Probably the most important single factor in the preparation of the employee is arousing and maintaining his interest. He must know the objectives of the training, why he is there, how the material can be used, and its importance to him.

2. Presentation

In presentation, have a carefully designed plan and follow it.
The plan should be accurate and complete, yet flexible enough to meet situations as they arise. The method of presentation will be determined by the particular situation and objectives.

3. Summary

A summary should be made at the end of every training unit and program. In addition, there may be internal summaries depending on the nature of the material being taught. The important thing is that the trainee must always be able to understand how each part of the new material relates to the whole.

4. Application

The supervisor must arrange work so the employee will be given a chance to apply new knowledge or skills while the material is still clear in his mind and interest is high. The trainee does not really know whether he has learned the material until he has been given a chance to apply it. If the material is not applied, it loses most of its value.

5. Evaluation

The purpose of all training is to promote learning. To determine whether the training has been a success or failure, the supervisor must evaluate this learning.
In the broadest sense evaluation includes all the devices, methods, skills, and techniques used by the supervisor to keep him self and the employees informed as to their progress toward the objectives they are pursuing. The extent to which the employee has mastered the knowledge, skills, and abilities, or changed his attitudes, as determined by the program objectives, is the extent to which instruction has succeeded or failed.
Evaluation should not be confined to the end of the lesson, day, or program but should be used continuously. We shall note later the way this relates to the rest of the teaching process.

B. Teaching Methods

A teaching method is a pattern of identifiable student and instructor activity used in presenting training material.
All supervisors are faced with the problem of deciding which method should be used at a given time.
As with all methods, there are certain advantages and disadvantages to each method.

1. Lecture

The lecture is direct oral presentation of material by the supervisor. The present trend is to place less emphasis on the trainer's activity and more on that of the trainee.

2. Discussion

Teaching by discussion or conference involves using questions and other techniques to arouse interest and focus attention upon certain areas, and by doing so creating a learning situation. This can be one of the most valuable methods because it gives the employees 'an opportunity to express their ideas and pool their knowledge.

3. Demonstration

The demonstration is used to teach how something works or how to do something. It can be used to show a principle or what the results of a series of actions will be. A well-staged demonstration is particularly effective because it shows proper methods of performance in a realistic manner.

4. Performance

Performance is one of the most fundamental of all learning techniques or teaching methods. The trainee may be able to tell how a specific operation should be performed but he cannot be sure he knows how to perform the operation until he has done so.

5. Which Method to Use

Moreover, there are other methods and techniques of teaching. It is difficult to use any method without other methods entering into it. In any learning situation a combination of methods is usually more effective than anyone method alone.

Finally, evaluation must be integrated into the other aspects of the teaching-learning process.

It must be used in the motivation of the trainees; it must be used to assist in developing understanding during the training; and it must be related to employee application of the results of training.

This is distinctly the role of the supervisor.

ANSWER SHEET

TEST NO. _____ PART _____ TITLE OF POSITION _____
(AS GIVEN IN EXAMINATION ANNOUNCEMENT - INCLUDE OPTION, IF ANY)

PLACE OF EXAMINATION _____ DATE _____
(CITY OR TOWN)   (STATE)

RATING

USE THE SPECIAL PENCIL.   MAKE GLOSSY BLACK MARKS.

Make only ONE mark for each answer.   Additional and stray marks may be counted as mistakes.   In making corrections, erase errors COMPLETELY.

ANSWER SHEET

TEST NO. ____________ PART ______ TITLE OF POSITION ____________________________
(AS GIVEN IN EXAMINATION ANNOUNCEMENT - INCLUDE OPTION, IF ANY)

PLACE OF EXAMINATION ______________________________ (CITY OR TOWN) ______________ (STATE) DATE ____________

RATING

USE THE SPECIAL PENCIL. MAKE GLOSSY BLACK MARKS.

1 A B C D E	26 A B C D E	51 A B C D E	76 A B C D E	101 A B C D E
2 A B C D E	27 A B C D E	52 A B C D E	77 A B C D E	102 A B C D E
3 A B C D E	28 A B C D E	53 A B C D E	78 A B C D E	103 A B C D E
4 A B C D E	29 A B C D E	54 A B C D E	79 A B C D E	104 A B C D E
5 A B C D E	30 A B C D E	55 A B C D E	80 A B C D E	105 A B C D E
6 A B C D E	31 A B C D E	56 A B C D E	81 A B C D E	106 A B C D E
7 A B C D E	32 A B C D E	57 A B C D E	82 A B C D E	107 A B C D E
8 A B C D E	33 A B C D E	58 A B C D E	83 A B C D E	108 A B C D E
9 A B C D E	34 A B C D E	59 A B C D E	84 A B C D E	109 A B C D E
10 A B C D E	35 A B C D E	60 A B C D E	85 A B C D E	110 A B C D E

Make only ONE mark for each answer. Additional and stray marks may be counted as mistakes. In making corrections, erase errors COMPLETELY.

11 A B C D E	36 A B C D E	61 A B C D E	86 A B C D E	111 A B C D E
12 A B C D E	37 A B C D E	62 A B C D E	87 A B C D E	112 A B C D E
13 A B C D E	38 A B C D E	63 A B C D E	88 A B C D E	113 A B C D E
14 A B C D E	39 A B C D E	64 A B C D E	89 A B C D E	114 A B C D E
15 A B C D E	40 A B C D E	65 A B C D E	90 A B C D E	115 A B C D E
16 A B C D E	41 A B C D E	66 A B C D E	91 A B C D E	116 A B C D E
17 A B C D E	42 A B C D E	67 A B C D E	92 A B C D E	117 A B C D E
18 A B C D E	43 A B C D E	68 A B C D E	93 A B C D E	118 A B C D E
19 A B C D E	44 A B C D E	69 A B C D E	94 A B C D E	119 A B C D E
20 A B C D E	45 A B C D E	70 A B C D E	95 A B C D E	120 A B C D E
21 A B C D E	46 A B C D E	71 A B C D E	96 A B C D E	121 A B C D E
22 A B C D E	47 A B C D E	72 A B C D E	97 A B C D E	122 A B C D E
23 A B C D E	48 A B C D E	73 A B C D E	98 A B C D E	123 A B C D E
24 A B C D E	49 A B C D E	74 A B C D E	99 A B C D E	124 A B C D E
25 A B C D E	50 A B C D E	75 A B C D E	100 A B C D E	125 A B C D E